Japan Today

Y
ES

KT-493-586

Japan Today

ROGER BUCKLEY

*Associate Professor of Political Science,
International Christian University, Tokyo*

SECOND EDITION

*The right of the
University of Cambridge
to print and sell
all manner of books
was granted by
Henry VIII in 1534.
The University has printed
and published continuously
since 1584.*

CAMBRIDGE UNIVERSITY PRESS

Cambridge

New York   Port Chester   Melbourne   Sydney

Published by the Press Syndicate of the University of Cambridge
The Pitt Building, Trumpington Street, Cambridge CB2 1RP
40 West 20th Street, New York, NY 10011, USA
10 Stamford Road, Oakleigh, Melbourne 3166, Australia

First published 1985
Reprinted 1987, 1988, 1989
This edition first published 1990
Reprinted 1990

Printed in Great Britain at the University Press, Cambridge

Library of Congress catalogue card number: 84–14300

British Library Cataloguing in Publication Data
Buckley, Roger
Japan today.
1. Japan – 2nd ed.
1. Title
952.04'8

ISBN 0 521 38238 6 hardback
ISBN 0 521 38885 6 paperback

First edition
ISBN 0 521 26089 2 hardback
ISBN 0 521 27832 5 paperback

For my parents and parents-in-law

We cannot become a truly international state unless we not only internationalize our economy but also make further progress in playing a positive global role culturally and politically.

Prime Minister Nakasone Yasuhiro, 10 September 1983

National character is something we all believe in, not so much because it really exists, as because to grasp the multifarious character of even one individual takes so much time, is such a trouble, is indeed so impossible, that we just put him together with a hundred million other unique individuals, and treat them all as one identical person.

R.H. Blyth, The 'Real' Japan

No – no – we know what the community wants; it wants something solid, it wants good wages, equal opportunities, good conditions of living, that's what the community wants. It doesn't want anything subtle or difficult. Duty is very plain – keep in mind the material, the immediate welfare of every man, that's all.

D.H. Lawrence, The Rainbow

Contents

Preface to the first edition

Any attempt to capture the essence of postwar Japan in a short survey must appear foolhardy. The only justification for my presumption is that recent, introductory works on contemporary Japan have been surprisingly rare and understandably cautious. There are, of course, many valuable analyses of the Japanese economy (frequently laudatory), its defence and external posture (or the lack of), present cultural and social relations (changing but with propriety) and domestic politics (Byzantine), but few observers have been reckless enough to gamble all on a general history. Reputations may be at risk. Still the effort deserves to be made – if only to provoke others to construct their superior version of reality.

Should any reader feel tempted by this sketch to consult some of the works listed in the short English-language bibliography he/she will immediately recognize the extent of my debts and inadequacies. The derivative nature of *Japan Today* is a tribute to others' scholarship. Space alone prevents the naming of the many individuals whose works I have ransacked for information and ideas. The resulting pot-pourri is my responsibility, not theirs. I must, however, pay thanks here to Professor Hosoya Chihiro and my colleagues at The International University of Japan for their tolerance of an acerbic European voice in their midst. My wife Machiko also deserves more than a mention for her assistance with translations, and understanding over forays to Tokyo. Lastly I have to thank Ms Jean Jenvey for typing up the manuscript and Ms Elizabeth Wetton for her editorial work.

Niigata-ken,
January 1984

Preface to the second edition

A chapter on developments concerning Japan since the mid-1980s has been added to the text, and the bibliography has been updated.

Mita
July 1989

Abbreviations

ACJ	Allied Council for Japan
ANZUS pact	Australia–New Zealand–United States Security Treaty
ASEAN	Association of South East Asian Nations
DSP	Democratic Socialist Party
EC	European Community
FEC	Far Eastern Commission
GATT	General Agreement on Tariffs and Trade
GNP	Gross National Product
JCP	Japan Communist Party
JNR	Japan National Railways
JSP	Japan Socialist Party
LDP	Liberal Democratic Party
MITI	Ministry of International Trade and Industry
MOF	Ministry of Finance
NATO	North Atlantic Treaty Organization
NHK	Japan Broadcasting Corporation
NLC	New Liberal Club
OPEC	Organization of Petroleum Exporting Countries
SCAP	Supreme Commander for the Allied Powers
SDF	Self-Defence Forces

Japanese names in the text follow Japanese convention with the family name placed before the given name.

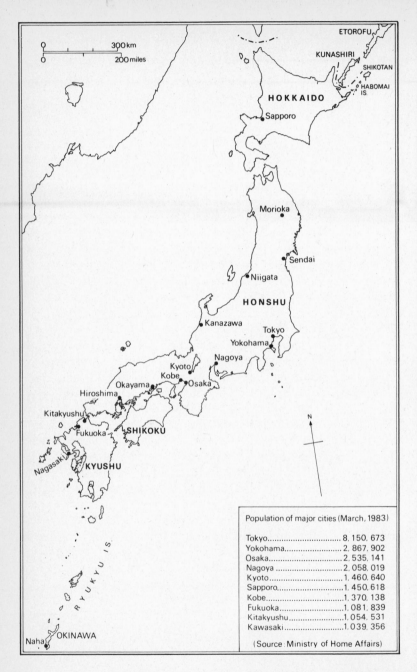

Population of major cities (March, 1983)

Tokyo	8,150,673
Yokohama	2,867,902
Osaka	2,535,141
Nagoya	2,058,019
Kyoto	1,460,640
Sapporo	1,450,618
Kobe	1,370,138
Fukuoka	1,081,839
Kitakyushu	1,054,531
Kawasaki	1,039,356

(Source: Ministry of Home Affairs)

Introduction

Japan is in the news. The evidence is apparent from a random examination of the North American and European press. To take but one example. During the summer of 1983 *The New York Times* ran no less than four major stories on Japan on the same morning. Its front page included a study of Japanese education and inside were articles on the continuing textbook controversy and two lengthy accounts of Japanese exporting zeal. The following month *Time* magazine would devote an entire issue to Japan, while the *Economist* had recently produced its own comparable survey. The Japanese diplomats and commentators who suggest that their nation is being neglected by the rest of the world have less cause for complaint today. Information abounds. What is sometimes lacking, however, is a more general framework to which the reader might attach this reportage. There is flesh aplenty but not always a skeleton. I have tried in this brief text to reduce what Japanese publicists are eager to term 'an obvious "communications" gap'.

New York, autumn 1982. Standing room only in the auditorium at Columbia. Long before the speaker was to be introduced the audience packed into the largest room the organizers could find. At last the meeting got underway, with the president of the international arm of Japan's leading securities company expounding on 'Japanese Style in Decision-Making'. The scene and title would have been unimaginable a decade earlier but similar presentations were now commonplace throughout the United States and Europe. Interest in Japan had suddenly become immense. Bookshops were replete with works on Japanese technology, Japanese business practices and even 17th-century Japanese folklore. Economists had a field-day. Journalists sensed potential best-sellers. The evidence was hard to refute. Mammoth exhibitions of Japanese art were mounted in London. John Updike reviewed Tanizaki. *Japan as Number One* was translated into Indonesian. The Duke of Edinburgh presented the Albert Medal to Morita Akio of Sony, while the British

1

government courted Japanese companies to build factories in South Wales or Merseyside. Even the inevitable backlash to some of the more overenthusiastic accounts of contemporary Japan received generous press coverage. The Japanese had clearly arrived. It was not stories of copycat radios or cheap porcelain that interested the public now but rather the latest range of video taperecorders and the fuel efficiency figures for Japanese cars. How did it happen? How does one explain Japan's rapid economic transformation and enduring social stability? This survey offers some clues.

'Japan's First Commercial Satellite Goes Up', 'General Motors and Toyota to co-produce a New Small Car in Fremont, California', 'Japanese Government to Take Clear Stand Against Export of Weapons', 'Japan Will Agree to US Blockade of its Straits'. These random headlines capture perhaps some of the energy, controversy and influence of today's Japan. Such indeed is Japan's economic power and growing international status that it would be difficult to deny the relevance of contemporary Japan for Western students of international relations and political economy. Japan has made itself an automatic selection. Its ability to survive relatively unscathed during the worst global depression since the 1930s is testimony to its economic strength and resilience, while the functioning of its political process is evidence of the maturity of Japan's democracy. Since Japan will not go away, it might be useful to move beyond the press reports and television clips to identify the nation's current strengths and weaknesses.

Japan Today attempts to describe and account for the more central features of Japan's present predicament. It assumes no previous knowledge or experience of Japan on the part of its readers. It is of necessity a primarily factual explanation of a nation of increasing importance to the rest of the world. A word next on what might be dressed up as methodology. It has remained a constant temptation both to employ gross generalizations on Japanese behaviour and alleged national character and to retreat to personal anecdotage to prove a case. All I can suggest in my defence is that readers might try explaining their own societies without endless reference to 'the English' or 'the Germans' and avoid travellers' tales when seemingly trumping an argument. It is not always easy. Still, this account of present day Japan is not intended to be a social science research monograph. It is written from a European perspective but without claim to membership of the rarefied, if inelegantly titled, profession of Japanology. Its theme will be less than welcome in some quarters, yet neglect of contemporary Japan could prove unfortunate. Without a more informed debate on its strengths and weaknesses the Western response is likely to lack conviction. The Japanese challenge may then turn into a rout.

The work is divided into six sections. The treatment is chronological and topical. It recognizes both the impact of the Allied occupation of Japan (1945–52) and more indigenous features behind Japan's rapid re-emergence as an international power. It will hopefully both show the positive factors behind Japan's recent 'success story' and point to the political and social problems which frequently receive less attention in popular versions of contemporary Japan. The intention is to avoid the hagiography of the *Japan as Number One* school and the equally misleading reverse image of a nation in permanent crisis. Rather Japan will be depicted as an essentially stable society – not forgetting its warts – that will continue to present an economic challenge to other industrialized states and will increasingly play a less diffident role in international affairs. One *caveat* at the outset. Those advocates of the Japanese experience who preach salvation for advanced industrialized states through learning from Japan will find little encouragement in this study. Given the social and historical configuration of Japan it is difficult to view the country as a model for others to emulate. What is good for Japan is not necessarily good for Ohio or the Ruhr. Different societies require different industrial organizations and strategies. Transplants rarely thrive.

To start with a truism. Japan's contemporary position can hardly be understood without some reference to its more immediate past. A complex society with a lengthy history and centuries of cultural homogeneity and linguistic unity deserves better than to have its present analysed in total isolation. Space restricts us to the briefest of discussions of the foundations of modern (post-1868) Japan. But constant note will be taken of Japan's wartime experiences (1937–45) and the occupation that followed its surrender, since postwar institutions and popular attitudes were strongly influenced by the traumas of defeat and occupation.

On 14 August 1945 the Pacific war ended in Japan's abject surrender. For a nation that had spent the preceding eight decades creating a modern state capable of gaining mastery of east Asia and the western Pacific it was the total negation of its recent history. The Meiji Restoration's aim of a 'rich country, strong army' had ended with a bankrupt state and a humiliated military. As the Emperor had explained, somewhat elliptically, in his imperial rescript of 14 August 'the war situation has developed not necessarily to Japan's advantage, while the general trends of the world have all turned against her interest'. The combination of the atomic bombing of Hiroshima and Nagasaki, the total US naval blockade of the Japanese archipelago and the Soviet declaration of war led to Japan's capitulation. It was, however, a close-run thing and the war might have continued but for the Emperor's unprecedented interventions at two imperial conferences. Further resistance was, of course, futile but to gain cabinet approval for surrender was no easy matter when the Vice-chief of the Naval General Staff could suggest on 13 August that 'if we are prepared to sacrifice 20,000,000 Japanese lives in a special attack [*kamikaze*] effort, victory shall be ours!' The vast casualties of the Pacific war and the mentality of Japan's military leaders remain fresh in the Japanese public's mind. Editorials on the anniversary of the horrific fire-bombings of Tokyo (9–10 March 1945) and the constant reference to the atomic destruction of Hiroshima (6 August 1945) suggest that this is not about to change. A widely shared distrust of Japan's hesitant postwar remilitarization stems from shared memories of the war and the austerity that followed. The road from Pearl Harbor led to pacifism.

1

Under reconstruction: the occupation and its legacy

The Allied occupation of Japan was the consequence of Japan's defeat in the Pacific war. It proved to be a determined, complex attempt to alter Japanese institutions and behaviour through a combination of 'dictation and persuasion'. It took place under American leadership against a changing international situation which led ultimately to a pro-Western peace treaty for Japan. The occupation was dominated by the United States since it had spearheaded the crushing of Japan and had rightly demanded that its forces predominate in the garrisoning of the captured home islands. Japan appeared initially to be a demoralized and bankrupt state with immense domestic problems and the added burden of accommodating itself to the wishes of its new rulers. It was an unenviable position but one which Western public opinion felt to be entirely of Japan's own making. The Japanese people seemed destined to receive some of the medicine they had meted out to their Asian neighbours. There was much talk of harsh reparations, strict economic blockade and the ignominy of the arraignment of the Emperor for his share of responsibility for Japan's recent appalling record.

The occupation, in reality, evolved differently from the wishes of Japan's harshest critics. This transpired for at least three reasons. It was clearly difficult for the United States to employ Carthaginian measures on a subjugated people once its crusade to destroy the Axis military had succeeded. Governments can have consciences. It was also against Washington's strategic self-interest to leave Japan destitute and open to possible intervention by the Soviet Union. Lastly, the generally co-operative, if unenthusiastic, response of the Japanese establishment to Allied designs tended to ameliorate Japan's predicament.

The first few months after Japan's formal surrender on 2 September 1945 proved to be crucial to Japan's future. The principal allies, having concurred in the appointment of General Douglas MacArthur as Supreme Commander for the Allied Powers (SCAP), discovered all too late that he and his government intended to embark on a programme of comprehensive reform. It was a remarkable bid to change permanently the face of Japanese life and prevent a repetition of the circumstances which led to the militarism that had so scarred the 1930s and contributed to the Pacific war. For senior American participants, the early part of the occupation was an exhilarating dawn marked by challenge, confusion and not a little success. For most Japanese it was less an occasion to rejoice. The rigours of eking out an existence in blitzed cities and overcrowded villages left little surplus energy for celebrating the 'New Japan'. The allies might be regarded in some quarters as liberators, but occupations, by definition, are almost invariably unpopular. It was more a question of accepting the inevitable in the expectation that this might speed up the process and lead to an early peace.

The choice of MacArthur as SCAP determined the character of much of the occupation's handiwork. MacArthur certainly received detailed orders from Washington but he contributed to the policy-making process by forwarding his own recommendations to the Army Department and the Joint Chiefs of Staff. While MacArthur was in general agreement with his nominal masters during the first three years of the period he had his own personal approach to Japanese questions. SCAP acknowledged that Japanese society might be capable of change if vigorous pressure were applied, but he was under no illusions as to the difficulties of making reform stick. He appreciated that Japan's long-term future would clearly be its own business – he wanted nothing to do with Allied supervisory bodies after a peace treaty had been signed – though he persisted in hoping that the occupation reforms might provide a firm foundation for a more democratic and liberal Japan.

MacArthur hoped, of course, that his proconsulate would not go unrecognized in the United States but Japan can consider itself fortunate in the choice of its occupation commander. MacArthur's approach to Japan was magnanimous in the main. SCAP intended to treat Japan in a manner which might lead to later more amicable US–Japan relations. He saw Tokyo as potentially of great value to his own nation. MacArthur had few friends in the United States or among the other Allied powers for much of this generosity. It was hardly good domestic politics in late 1945 to insist on the retention of the Emperor, to obtain scarce food imports, to disown reparation recommendations and to consider an early resumption of foreign trade. MacArthur supported, however, the purge programme, particularly of Japanese army officers, and agreed with the establishment of the International Military Tribunal for the Far East to try suspected war criminals. He was also in favour of reducing the power of the Zaibatsu, the prewar combines, and hoped that non-political trades unions might be encouraged to act as a countervailing power to these Japanese business groups. MacArthur's political sympathies were with the moderate left, despite his own Republican presidential aspirations, though the vagaries of occupation politics ultimately obliged him to deal for most of this period with Yoshida Shigeru, an elderly conservative politician who had a chequered prewar diplomatic career.

The intellectual origins of the Allied occupation and the Japanese contribution to the outcome deserve mention at this point. SCAP GHQ was a military organization but some of its more influential officials were civilians. This created some tension between personnel who had held responsible administrative posts in New Deal agencies and the stauncher conservatives who tended to regard anti-Communism as an integral part of their mission in Japan. There were bitter debates between the reformist groups in General Whitney's Government Section and those eager to adopt a Cold War perspective in General Willoughby's G–2 (Intelligence) branch. Willoughby exchanged cigars for sherry with General Franco every Christmas. The more frequent victor in these ideological disputes was Whitney, though MacArthur himself could and did intervene on occasion to overrule his favoured staff. Allied and Japanese access to even the fringe of these policy meetings was difficult. The best prospect for unofficial representation was to build up a store of goodwill with MacArthur himself, or, failing that, with his senior aides. Use of more public forums such as the Allied Council for Japan (ACJ), which met regularly in Tokyo, or the Far Eastern Commission (FEC), which led a frustrating existence in Washington, rarely ended happily. MacArthur never liked to deal with either international body and made no secret of his antipathy towards what he interpreted as unwarranted interference. MacArthur's inner circle largely ran the show in the early years of the occupation. The British prime minister's personal representative to SCAP saw later that 'MacArthur *was* Japan' (his italics) and spoke of having been in attendance at 'the court of MacArthur'. Yoshida, who also met the supreme commander regularly, employed various tactics to gain an airing for his views. One technique was to leave behind unsigned memoranda after interviews with MacArthur. Yoshida, who regarded much of the reformist character of the occupation with the utmost suspicion, was not afraid to confront GHQ with his doubts. Indeed, it is difficult to think of any occupation legislation which had Yoshida's active blessing.

He appreciated, however, that Allied land reform had saved the countryside from Communism, even though Yoshida was more interested after 1952 in demolishing sensitive parts of MacArthur's handiwork than consolidating or extending its ethos.

Yoshida's relations with MacArthur typified much of the Japanese official response to the occupation. It was, at times, less a question of the United States imposing its will on Japan than attempting to gain its co-operation in order to carry through its designs. Given the indirect nature of American rule (a vital and correct decision in the circumstances), there were frequent opportunities for Japanese bureaucrats and politicians at all levels of government either to inject a sense of urgency into a multitude of new programmes or quietly to stymie the process. The occupation was more often government by Japanese interpreter and official than American command; it could hardly be otherwise once the reform legislation became law. The further one went from Tokyo the more this became apparent. The pressing need to increase coal production might be recognized by all in SCAP GHQ and Yoshida's cabinet but miners in Hokkaido could hold a different view of Japan's plight. Similarly, local factors determined the extent to which well-intentioned labour reforms or taxation changes were actually put into practice. The occupation should not be seen as operating exclusively under a metropolitan dictat. Prefectural governors and village headmen often had the final say.

The United States' intentions in Japan were little short of revolutionary. It intended to reshape vast areas of Japanese life on the strength of its confidence in the blessings of American institutions, which had seemingly brought about Japan's recent total defeat and unconditional surrender. The United States' planners for postwar Japan believed that Japanese society was ripe for radical change (preferably on American lines) in its constitutional, industrial and social patterns. It was an absurdly ambitious programme, which sceptics at home and abroad thought doomed to failure. Secretary Stimson, drawing probably on his experiences as the Senior American official in the Philippines, advised Truman in July 1945:

I would hope that our occupation of the Japanese islands would not involve the government of the country as a whole in any such manner as we are committed in Germany. I am afraid we would make a hash of it if we tried. The Japanese are an oriental people with an oriental mind and religion. Our occupation should be limited to that necessary to (a) impress the Japanese, and the orient as a whole, with the fact of Japanese defeat, (b) demilitarize the country, and

(c) punish war criminals, including those responsible for the perfidy of Pearl Harbor.

British thinking, influenced by the reputation of the Japanologist Sir George Sansom, followed in very much the same cautious vein. But planners in Washington thought otherwise and gained presidential approval for a quite remarkable set of instructions. MacArthur was ordered by the United States Initial Post-Surrender Policy for Japan to make certain that Japan remained unable to pose a security threat to the United States and its Allies and that a 'peaceful' and 'responsible government' acting true to 'the principles of democratic self-government' was deemed desirable. To achieve these objectives 'the Japanese people shall be encouraged to develop a desire for individual liberties and respect for fundamental human rights, particularly the freedoms of religion, assembly, speech, and the press. They shall also be encouraged to form democratic and representative organisations'. Lastly, 'democratic political parties, with rights of assembly and public discussion were to be promoted and 'the judicial, legal, and police systems shall be reformed . . . to protect individual liberties and civil rights'.

There remained one important qualification. MacArthur was told that the new Japanese government 'should conform as closely as may be to principles of democratic self-government but it is not the responsibility of the Allied Powers to impose upon Japan any form of Government not supported by the freely expressed will of the people'. There was, therefore, from the first days of the occupation, a built-in contradiction in the approach to be followed towards Japan. It was far from clear how this tension would be resolved if, for example, the Japanese government, in its wisdom, were to resist the forced importation of Western democratic institutions and practices. Differences were soon apparent over a wide front.

The most convenient starting place for discussion of occupation reform is the 1947 constitution. It remains the foundation of the whole Allied edifice and yet continues to engender controversy. Much of the criticism later directed at the constitution can best be appreciated by examining the manner in which the document was written. The truth may be uncomfortable, but the postwar constitution was imposed upon Japan by the United States largely against the wishes of the Japanese government and its advisers. A small number of Japanese amendments were permitted by SCAP GHQ, but the constitution was an American formulation designed in the early months of 1946 to forestall the possibility that the FEC might present its own rival version. The constitution was less the child of the Cold War than the product of American unilateralism.

The Japanese and Allied gradualists who had felt that modification of the existing Meiji constitution might suffice were decisively beaten. The new document was concocted from disparate sources to provide a two chamber legislature with cabinet government on the British model. Supporters of the new constitution could claim that the process was a logical extension of 'Taisho Democracy'. It was maintained that precisely defined and greatly enhanced powers for both the executive and legislature (including an elaborate American committee structure), and the provision of female suffrage, an independent judiciary and a bill of rights were but the inevitable climax to democratic forces already existing within Japanese society.

This argument is not entirely persuasive. It tends to ignore the weaknesses of earlier attempts at parliamentary government and the mild repression of the war years. Left to itself the Japanese establishment would never have risked a constitution as radical as that imposed on Japan in 1946–7. Without arm-twisting and reminders of American military strength postwar Japanese politics would have taken a different road; conservative forces would have regrouped to swamp less reactionary elements even in the months following Japan's defeat. The new constitution was an alien import. It spoke of the individual's goals as 'life, liberty, and the pursuit of happiness' (article 13) and had to inform the Japanese public that the 'fundamental human rights by this Constitution guaranteed to the people of Japan are fruits of the age-old struggle of man to be free' (article 97). It was inevitably difficult to work up much enthusiasm for a document first drafted in English and drawn from a different political culture. Only gradually over the following decades did the constitution gain in popularity. It would, however, be dangerous to regard as conclusive the argument of its supporters that the constitution has proved itself since no amendments have yet been forthcoming. Such thinking ignores the immense difficulties of the amendment procedure. Constitutional amendments require a two-thirds vote of approval in each house of the Diet followed by a simple majority in a popular referendum. No cabinet would risk entering this area without being confident of victory. Attempts to alter the constitutional position of the Emperor or to revise the 'no-war' clause of article 9 seem unlikely to succeed in the foreseeable future, although elements within the ruling Liberal Democratic Party remain eager for change.

Under the Meiji constitution the issue of where sovereignty lay had been unclear. In theory it resided with the Emperor, whose position has been variously described as ideologically absolutist and anti-modern. Such a view was promoted by the presentation of the 1889 constitution as a gift from the Emperor to his grateful subjects. Since the Emperor appointed the government he was the state. Later additions during the Meiji era left the political structure of Japan capable of being manipulated to extol the virtues of patriotism, filial piety and hierarchy. In reality sovereignty was located elsewhere. By the 1930s it was apparent that the military, assisted by political and bureaucratic forces, had won control of the Japanese state. It was in order to prevent any possible pre-emption in the future that the elaborate postwar constitution was propounded. Despite the hopes of some in SCAP GHQ it was likely that the forces of tradition would retain power after Japan's surrender in 1945. This had two effects. It made a radically different constitution essential to give encouragement to left-wing parties and trades unionists so that they would no longer be precluded from influencing their nation's future. Yet this involvement by Japan's left led also to exaggerated popular expectations of its ability to solve their country's problems, and contributed to rapid disillusionment with the non-conservative groups when given the unexpected opportunity to govern.

The failure of the Socialist-led coalition under Katayama Tetsu in 1947 was something of a foregone conclusion, since it had little prospect of containing – let alone solving – a difficult economic situation, yet it was under popular pressure to assume office and be seen to support democratic measures. It did little to enhance the electoral prospects for democratic socialism but much for the new constitution. It may have been political suicide but it was a necessary attempt to forge a responsible left-wing government. Katayama's unsuccessful period in office has proved to be the Socialists' only taste of power. The 1949 election returns confirmed the uphill problems which the left has had to confront since the occupation. It remains equally true today that, in the words of one disillusioned former Government Section official who had encouraged the Socialists, 'the prospects for a two-party system in Japan are poor simply because there is no group which can effectively oppose the formidable old guard conservatives'.

Consideration of the Emperor's position was vital to the progress of the occupation. It was also certain to generate controversy. Allied governments and the media had debated his future at length during the war and could be relied on to possess firm opinions as to his fate. At its crudest the issue was whether to arraign the Emperor for his nominal (or real) responsibility for Japan's expansionism or to employ him to further the aims of the Allies. It was decided by the United States government, with the eager support of MacArthur in Tokyo and the British Foreign Office in its representations to Washington, that the Emperor be retained. It was the only appropriate decision, unless the Allies were prepared to reckon with the consequences – possibly violent – of removing the head of the Japanese state in whose name the imperial forces had fought and died.

By the time the new constitution was promulgated the Emperor's worth had been widely recognized by Allied diplomats, though this did not prevent influential voices from calling for his indictment at the Tokyo war-crimes trials. The Emperor was retained but he was largely stripped of his prewar influence. He was no longer to be head of state, becoming instead merely the 'symbol of state'. His duties were ceremonial and precisely enumerated. MacArthur made the Emperor call on him and thereafter closely watched his activities. Thus, the Emperor's position in Japanese public life gradually changed. Today it is apparent that respect for his personage has greatly decreased among the postwar generations, although republicanism is not around the corner. The palace is required to perform a series of largely routine functions, which it undertakes with stiff dignity, before a variously respectful or indifferent populace. The Emperor and his successors seem likely to provide a sense of unity and continuity to some elements in Japanese society.

The two most important reforms after the new constitution had been drafted concerned agriculture and education. First land reform. This was instituted as much for political as economic ends. The highly ambitious aim was to create a new rural society where tenant farmers would be replaced by freeholders. MacArthur, pushing somewhat a false comparison between the United States of his youth and postwar Japan, intended that the sharecropper should be replaced by an independent yeomanry. The expectation was that the tenancy rows of the interwar years and the desperate poverty of large parts of the countryside might be avoided in the future by permitting all who so wished to purchase their own land. Absentee landlordism would be virtually outlawed and its political and economic influence destroyed for good. Strict limits were to be placed on the acreage allowed to any single farmer's household. SCAP intended to remove what it saw as the root cause of much prewar bitterness and political extremism, since all too often a Tohoku peasant in the 1930s had discovered that life in the Imperial Army, despite its undoubted hardship, proved a less brutal calling than scratching an existence in northern Japan. The accretion of a little seniority made the discipline and regimentation of the army easier to bear. Junior officers were also thought to have been particularly sympathetic to the plight of their men's rural communities and eager to obtain a better deal for the countryside.

To be fair then to the Japanese establishment, there were prewar precedents for parts of SCAP's land programme. But it would have been asking too much of this group to imagine that it would have voluntarily activated a scheme as radical as that ordered by SCAP. The occupation's land reforms (partly the handiwork of Australia and a rare example of harmony in the ACJ) meant that the prewar landlords had to accept the virtual expropriation of their fields. Compensation was far from generous, but at least Japan was spared the bloodshed which was to mark similar reforms in China after 1949. Elimination of the Chinese gentry as a class was rarely accomplished in the Japanese manner of mixed farmer and landlord committees. The demise of the prewar landlords left the way open for new political forces and personalities to make their appearance in the countryside.

The role of agriculture has evolved rapidly since the days when the demobbed Japanese soldier returned home to his village. The importance of agriculture as a major component of the Japanese economy has greatly diminished. The severity of the occupation's reforms left farmers with extremely small plots and the lure of new industrial jobs further depleted the stock of younger people prepared to put in the backbreaking work required to grow wet paddy rice. Today agriculture is in danger of becoming little more than a part-time job for the elderly.

Political and economic reforms were easier to institute than attempts to alter the social structure of occupied Japan. Many commentators thought this very concept of promoting a mass change of heart absurdly overambitious. As with other Allied schemes, the aim was to move fast before prewar forces might re-assert themselves and to present alternative models and constituents that could fight off the temporarily discredited old ways. But Imperial Japan could not be instantly erased from history. Those who had been brought up in the Meiji period and returning soldiers who had expected to die for the Emperor were not easily convinced that democracy, equality and freedom were necessarily superior concepts. Besides, the poverty and uncertainty facing most

Japanese after the war left limited opportunities for rethinking the past. Some occupation authorities recognized that it was hardly an auspicious time to call for a great experiment. SCAP persisted. Evidence that the going would be hard was readily apparent. Public respect for the Emperor when he began his provincial inspection tours contrasted sharply with the lack of interest in the progress of the Tokyo war-crimes trials (the International Military Tribunal for the Far East). Memories were selective. With the Japanese family the inevitable centre of most people's lives at a time when individual resources were hopelessly inadequate, it was probably asking too much to expect more than lip service paid to new roles for mothers and daughters or any substantial encouragement to younger sons to fend for themselves. Individualism and personal mobility were the last things a hardpressed family needed to hear of. Women might get and use the vote, but their husbands frequently assumed that political equality ought not to impinge on masculine privileges. The content of education and the organization of the school system might change, but most of the old teachers remained. Values and beliefs could be altered only with difficulty.

Sceptical British observers foresaw that the results of educational reforms could hardly be gauged until the first generation of schoolchildren taught under the new scheme had reached maturity. Yet, as in other fields, such British and Commonwealth thinking was more than occasionally jaundiced. A start had to be made or the momentum would be lost. The re-organization of education was not without its problems, but it was a bold venture that permanently removed the ultra-nationalistic flavour of earlier Japanese schooling. Textbooks were rewritten, curricula revised, decentralization encouraged and the entire structure of education from primary school to university rejigged. The new system was to have its share of critics in the coming years, but it is doubtful if the ideological preferences of the Allies could have gained ground without such comprehensive reform. The United States, through the advice of its specialist Education Mission to Japan and the Civil Information and Education Staff section of SCAP GHQ, saw the conflict over the content and organization of education as the key to moulding a new Japan. It was one American 'hearts and minds' campaign that did pay off.

The Allies' motive for altering the prewar industrial–financial combines (Zaibatsu) was clear cut. The economic strength of the four largest Zaibatsu (Mitsui, Mitsubishi, Sumitomo and Yasuda) was widely recognized to be unhealthy by those in SCAP GHQ wishing to promote economic democracy. The reputation of the Zaibatsu overseas and the belief that Japan's continental aggression was the result of an unholy alliance between big business and the military ensured that change was inevitable after 1945. The Zaibatsu had their fingers in too many pies to remain unscathed. A few select families dominated a few large combines, which in turn had a hammerlock on whole sectors of the Japanese economy. The system was controlled through the Zaibatsu banks. The big four employed financial obligations and personnel transfers to keep their subsidiaries and subcontractors in line. Half the financial business (banking, insurance and credit) and one-third of Japan's heavy industries were under Zaibatsu control in 1942. To the Manchester liberal and the Washington trustbuster this was all anathema.

Economic reform on the scale envisaged by some American officials would never have been introduced, but for the importance of the Zaibatsu to Japan's war effort and their close ties to senior bureaucrats and political circles. In 1947 seemingly tough antimonopoly and deconcentration legislation was approved by the Japanese Diet at the insistence of the United States. It appeared that there were to be structural changes to Japan's economy to deprive the old Zaibatsu families and groups of their former power. But the changes turned out to be considerably more modest than some had hoped. The family influence largely disappeared, but the shifts in American foreign policy towards east Asia following the evident collapse of Nationalist China and calls from the Congress to guard against unnecessary spending overseas left the core of Japanese finance and industry unimpaired. After 1949, Japanese reconstruction was more important than Allied retribution. The old combines regrouped and returned to something akin to their former status. Japan's postwar economic progress would have been severely hampered if SCAP's original curtailment programme had remained intact.

Valuable accounts of the contemporary Japanese economy have been written that exclude all reference to trades unions. To British readers, aware that union membership of their coal and railway industries comprises 100% of the labour force, this is difficult to comprehend. Yet Japanese industrial relations, for all their seeming differences and relative unimportance in Japanese society, deserve more than passing mention. Once again our starting point will be the occupation.

Initial American policies towards reviving and encouraging Japanese trades unions were in keeping with its aims of creating a new series of Japanese institutions which might counterbalance the old order. Unions had existed before the war, but their leaders had continually faced opposition from the police and industrialists. All this was to change with the arrival of experienced American labour activists and advisers. A host of legislative reforms, including the establishment of Japan's first Labour Ministry and pro-union laws, were introduced in the next two years. Unionization followed rapidly in most industries, although the benefits won by the workers were in constant danger of being wiped out by the hyperinflation of the period. The politicization of the new unions, which ultimately resulted in MacArthur banning a general strike hours before it was due to begin on 1 February 1947, was less to the liking of the United States. Changes in labour law, including restrictions on the activities of industrial civil servants who had been in the vanguard of strike calls, followed. Such acts – regressive in the view of the British and Australian governments – reduced the influence of important sections of the labour movement. Yet, despite these and later curtailments, the occupation's record deserves praise. Japan's labour unions, notwithstanding bitter feuding between rival left-wing groups and a strong tendency to organize on enterprise rather than industrial lines, had come of age by 1952.

Japan regained its independence with the ratification of the Treaty of San Francisco signed in 1952 after an occupation that had lasted from the summer of 1945 until April 1952. It was by any standards a remarkable period of cultural contrasts, changing policies and considerable accomplishment. The occupation era – yet to find its historian – is difficult to summarize. Much of the American literature tends to be written from entrenched positions, while Japanese commentators have been discouraged by the timidity of the Japanese government in releasing official documents and by the myriad conflicting memories that the occupation continues to arouse. To give one sensational but typical example: a recent Japanese reconstruction of Yoshida's role during these years begins with GIs committing multiple rape, attacking senior Japanese bureaucrats and desecrating the flag. Television has a lot to answer for. With the Japanese public being reminded of the brutality and hunger of the occupation and the United States looking instead at its own generosity and idealism, it is not easy to envisage any future meeting of minds. Part of the occupation's legacy has been to leave very different national recollections of what the process was intended to do and how it was carried out. International understanding at this level remains a dream.

To return briefly to the international context of the occupation. Many critics of American policy in Japan held that the occupation ran out of steam long before 1952. General MacArthur had suggested as early as March 1947 that Japan had faithfully carried out its surrender obligations and the British government made similar representations to the State Department on numerous occasions. There would appear to be little doubt that it was American fears of Japan's economic and strategic vulnerability that delayed progress towards any Allied peace settlement. The onset of the Cold War and the strength of Communist forces in east and southeast Asia cautioned the American administration from letting Japan have a free hand. The eventual peace treaty had a quite definite quid pro quo attached to it. Japan was obliged to consent to the US–Japan Security Treaty on the same day that it signed the San Francisco documents. The left in Japan protested vehemently that this new military alliance had been dictated by Washington to perpetuate the occupation.

Under the terms of the peace treaty, Japan, at the behest largely of the United States, was granted peace that reflected the overall tone of the occupation. It was a generous settlement. Its critics felt it was unnecessarily forgiving and let Japan off too easily. Although Japanese sentiment did not view it quite so favourably – there was public dissatisfaction over the territorial clauses with respect to four small northern islands off Hokkaido (part of the Kurile chain) and the American retention of Okinawan bases – there was relief that the business was now over. The Japanese public, feeling that the occupation had been uncomfortably prolonged to fit their nation into the United States' Pacific security schemes, wanted only to get on with the job of rebuilding its economy. Reconstruction seemingly had no place for talk of re-armament and international responsibilities.

It was, however, impossible for the Japanese government to bury its head completely in the sand. A nation with Japan's recent record, its present human resources and future potential to regain its industrial position could hardly expect plain sailing. Like it or not, Japan remerged after 1952 as a ward of the United States. But not even Washington could prevent the other Pacific powers from voicing considerable concern over where Japan might be going. Australia and New Zealand were only mollified by the creation of the Australia–New

Zealand–United States Security Treaty (ANZUS pact), which gave guarantees that aggression in the Pacific would be resisted by the United States. Similar promises were contained in the US–Philippines defence agreement, while Manila and the rest of Asia that had known the Japanese heel were eager to gain all they could from later protracted reparation negotiations.

The San Francisco conference also had a number of empty chairs. Indonesia did not sign, though it made a separate accord later. India sat on the fence, since it wanted to lead what would shortly be termed the Third World and had no wish to antagonize its Himalayan neighbours. But a greater defect was the absence of any Chinese delegation. This was caused by the impossibility of an agreement between Britain and the United States on which of the two Chinese governments might be invited to the proceedings. It was an unsatisfactory face-saving compromise that was resolved shortly afterwards when Japan signed a treaty with Taiwan. The Soviet Union surprisingly attended but then predictably rejected the Anglo-American treaty terms.

One continually voiced fear by practically all participants and non-signatories alike was the danger of future Japanese expansionism. The United States government insisted that the rise of Nazism had demonstrated the impossibility of writing military restrictions into peace treaties. John Foster Dulles, the leader of the American team to San Francisco and the architect of the Japanese peace settlements, had attended the Versailles conference in 1919 and was frequently to recall the failures of the Allies' plans to contain postwar Germany. Ultimately, Dulles argued, the San Francisco powers could only trust Japan not to re-arm in depth. It was an act of faith based on the twin assumptions that Japan had learnt its lesson and that the reconstruction of the Japanese economy and opportunities for international trade would more than compensate for its loss of empire. Events have so far proved Dulles right. Japan's energies since the occupation have been channelled into developing an economic structure that is the envy of less successful nations. The tensions which currently exist with Japan's trading partners over its economic performance will be discussed later.

Japan in 1952 was once more an independent sovereign state. It could be reasonably certain that the United States would continue to assist financially and ensure the safety of the Japanese islands. Washington was simply unwilling to consider the possibility of letting Japan go its own way, since the strategic and industrial might of Japan (even the diminished Japan of 1952) was a vital factor in the United

States' Pacific security system. To make this clear to friend and foe alike, the US–Japan Security Treaty permitted the deployment of American forces 'in and about Japan so as to deter armed attack upon Japan' and, if called upon by Tokyo, 'to put down large-scale internal riots and disturbances in Japan, caused through instigation or intervention by an outside power or powers'. American base areas appeared to many Japanese to have some of the unpleasant characteristics of the unequal treaties imposed on Japan in the mid-19th century. It smacked of imperialism. Yet given Japan's own reluctance to re-arm (Yoshida had prevaricated when Dulles pressed him to give a firm commitment) and the realities of east Asian international relations (the Korean war brought this home to sections of the Japanese public), there were few American alternatives. Hopes that Japan might gradually take over more of the responsibilities for its own defence were only partly realized later.

2

Japan's political environment

The conservatives run Japan. Government is firmly in their hands and has been so since 1948. Domination on this scale by similar political groupings for over 35 years is unique among the world's democracies (although in Australia the conservative Liberal Party was in power for 23 years to 1972). The pattern did not begin with the occupation – Japan's prewar governments had civilian elements which reflected conservative business and landlord strengths in the country – but the ability of traditionalist politicians to attract mass support despite their implication in the Pacific war deserves notice. Commentators have to explain how the conservatives gained power after the surrender and then, with the exception of a brief period in 1947–8, confidently retained their grip. By the 1980s their dominance was such as to leave little doubt that the opposition parties faced a seemingly endless period in the shadows unless the right should split irreparably. Cold comfort for the left.

The first years of the occupation were clearly a period of great political uncertainty. The intentions of the United States were liable to change and the volatility of the electorate further increased the difficulties of rival parties. There was much talk of how Japan must reform itself and aspire to uphold democratic values. There was also an undercurrent of contradictory rhetoric which stressed the need to maintain Japanese values when facing a lengthy occupation.

There were important continuities as well as sharp contrasts with the Japan that had fought in China from 1937 and then waged war on the Allies. In politics the campaign slogans might suggest a new order but prewar politicians, bureaucrats, diplomats and labour leaders soon re-appeared. All had to pay close attention to the hints and commands of SCAP GHQ, while demonstrating their ability to organize and mount campaigns for office. Some aspirants were simply purged by MacArthur's staff when their earlier records were examined, but the Japanese POW who had predicted to his Allied interrogator that 'unless you run the country from top to bottom for a generation, which is not exactly democratic either, you will have to take what co-operation you can find and not be too particular about it' was surely correct. SCAP had to work with whoever emerged from the wash. It could only manipulate so far, if it wished to profess adherence to the ballot box. The consequences were decidedly messy.

The initial post-surrender cabinet was headed by the Emperor's cousin. After Higashikuni's departure there followed three years of political musical chairs. Governments came and went without much success in solving the economic problems which engulfed the nation. Although parties changed names and leaders without turning a hair, there is little evidence to suggest anyone was equipped to take the unpopular decisions needed to salvage something from the wreck. Conservative cabinets by former diplomats – presumed to be able to ingratiate themselves with their American overlords – were as weak as the succeeding coalitions of the centre and moderate left. Only in the elections of January 1949 did the electorate give a clear indication of its preference. Yoshida Shigeru was returned to power with an absolute majority. The conservative hue of Japanese politics was now quite definite. Yoshida's Democratic Liberal Party swamped its rivals and ended the period of fluctuation and hesitancy. It would be relatively easy to argue that this was all on the cards and that the conservatism of the Japanese electorate was never in doubt, despite the 'reign of terror' instigated by SCAP. But it was not as simple as that. A more adventurous display by centralist groups and a less openly defiant stance by some labour unions might have made it harder going for Yoshida. He was, after all, far less popular in Allied circles than he led himself to believe. His emergence as Japan's leader – brought about initially by the purge of his party boss – was, however, fully apparent following his 1949 triumph.

Yoshida dominated Japanese politics during and after the occupation. His influence, through what became known as the 'Yoshida School', lived on long after his demise. Yoshida had an abrasive personality and was not frightened to speak out against what he saw as American errors in running the occupation. This earned him some respect from MacArthur and a degree of popularity from the Japanese public. With the conclusion of the peace treaty, his combativeness, while appreciated when Japan was prostrate, became increasingly distasteful. Yoshida, however, did not fade away. He clung to power, although challenged by rivals, including Hatoyama Ichiro, who had appeared certain to be premier in 1946 until suddenly purged by SCAP. Eventually in November 1954 Yoshida was obliged to resign. It was something of a fiasco at the end but Yoshida's reputation would later revive. If his last years in office were inglorious, his 'one man' legend appears secure. Yoshida is the only Japanese politician to have made it to Madame Tussaud's and immortality in wax.

Yoshida's departure was followed by major re-alignments in conservative ranks in order to ward off a reorganization of socialist forces. The challenge from the left spurred the Liberals (Yoshida's men) and Democrats (under Hatoyama) to unite in November 1955 as the Liberal Democratic Party (LDP). Under this title the conservative coalition of disparate factions has held uninterrupted power. It is indeed the case that the LDP 'knows only how to govern'. Despite talk of oppositional unity – rarely more than talk given the ideological differences which would have to be papered over – the conservatives have sailed on. A long procession of scandals, factional knuckle fights and threats of walkouts have not been permitted to destroy the façade of unity that enables the party to win election after election. How this is achieved we shall see later.

In the 1950s political battles were fought largely over foreign policy. The left argued that the very peace treaty that had ended the Allied occupation was in itself a disguised form of continued American domination. The security arrangement, whereby Japan agreed to the stationing of American forces throughout its islands, was widely interpreted as an unequal treaty which refuted Japanese government claims that Tokyo had regained its national sovereignty. American bases appeared to perpetuate the occupation. The occasional unguarded comment by American spokesmen that the United States had not only to protect Japan but to protect the Pacific region from Japan tended to confirm the opposition in the justice of its complaints. It campaigned vigorously for the termination of the US–Japan Security Treaty. Incidents involving American military personnel and Japanese civilians were a source of major embarrassment to both governments.

Successive conservative cabinets attempted to walk a precarious path between American insistence that Japan begin to re-arm in more than token style and a widespread popular revulsion against remilitarization. This pacifism was not the exclusive property of the Communists and Socialists. Many on the right shared these sentiments, albeit for somewhat less clearcut ideological motives. Business federations saw little advantage in diverting scarce resources to non-productive enterprises. Many of their supporters took the pragmatic (and very Japanese) position that defeat in the Pacific war had led Japan up a blind alley. Japan's mistake was to lose. It could now best fulfil its destiny by regaining its economic strength.

Popular agreement that Japan's first priority had to be the re-establishment of a firm economic structure played immediately into the hands of the LDP. The party of business claimed that it could be safely left with the task of restoring Japan's economy. The evidence was soon apparent. Already by 1954 the prewar peak year of 1939 had been surpassed for GNP. The years that followed quickly demonstrated the conservatives' skill at maximizing production. Double digit growth became the norm throughout most of the 1950s and 1960s. The press in Japan and abroad began to talk of 'economic miracles'. The opposition had a poor hand to play against this newly gained prosperity. Its strongest suit was re-armament.

The left was ever-vigilant against what it interpreted as dangerous signs of nascent remilitarism. It deplored, as we have seen, the San Francisco peace settlements and sharply criticized the creation of the Defence Agency in 1954. The influence of the United States in the organization and material of the Japanese ground, maritime and air self-defence forces was an additional charge to be employed against the government. The US Army Area Handbook for Japan could note 'the components of Japan's military establishment in 1960 resemble their counterparts in the United States Armed Forces in miniature'. (It was all a far cry from the days when French artillery advisers and Royal Navy officers had assisted at the birth of the Meiji armed forces in the 1870s and 1880s.) The left instead spoke of unarmed neutrality as a substitute for the LDP's pro-American defence and foreign policies. It set its sights on an end to the US–Japan Security Treaty, which was due to be renegotiated in 1960. The conservatives were well aware of the dangers they faced over defence. It was an unpopular issue with their own supporters, let alone the opposition groups. Public anxiety over Japan's limited freedom of action as an American ally during a period of intense East–West strain made it essential that the government gain a greater say in American strategic thinking for its Japanese bases. The result was the most serious political crisis in the first two decades of the post-San Francisco era.

The ensuing turmoil overshadowed the earlier domestic achievements of the LDP's premier Kishi Nobusuke and led to his resignation after he had forced the revised security pact through the Diet. Street demonstrations led to violence, parliamentary tactics ended in brawls, the American president's press secretary was roughed up, and a female student from Tokyo University was trampled to death. Kishi, who had the rug pulled from under him by rival LDP factions eager to gain his downfall, was criticized from all sides. He had, however, won considerable concessions from the United States that made the security treaty less unequal.

The years since Kishi's departure have been relatively calm. The political climate changed after the 1960 treaty had been digested. Kishi's successors, Ikeda Hayato and Sato Eisaku, were determined to emphasize Japan's continuing economic achievements and to play down the more controversial fields of foreign and defence policies. Both wished to maintain close relations with the United States, without provoking the opposition to organize the mass demonstrations that had obliged Kishi to cancel President Eisenhower's proposed visit to Tokyo in June 1960.

Not until the jolts of President Nixon's twin 'shocks' in 1971, which altered the role of the dollar in international trade and led to his visit to Peking, was the American connection re-assessed by the conservatives. Yet for all the critical editorials and parliamentary debate that these two measures aroused by the absence of prior consultation between Washington and Tokyo, it was to be economic dangers which belatedly brought home to the Japanese people its international vulnerability. The Arab–Israeli war of October 1973 was quickly seen as the end of an era. The high growth years became a thing of the past. The Japanese government under the leadership of Tanaka Kakuei, a horsedealer's son who had made a fortune in the construction industry, was beset by difficulties. The oil embargo hurt. Industry passed on its increased costs to consumers. Labour pressed for substantial wage increases. Inflation soared. The self-confidence of the government and the public at large was badly dented. It was a critical period by any standards. The issue was more intractable than forcing Kishi to resign or putting pressure on the United States to return Okinawa. The basis of Japan's entire postwar prosperity appeared to be in doubt.

Yet the government held. For all the gross profiteering of business sectors and panic hoarding by housewives, the conservatives were able to ride out the storm. The Tanaka cabinet, largely through the efforts of the premier's rival, Fukuda Takeo, was able gradually to dampen down the inflationary fires, though inevitably at the cost of double digit growth. Plans for greater pollution control, improved urban environments, and regional rather than metropolitan priorities were quietly shelved for the interim. Those economists who had been confidently predicting 8%–10% annual growth rates until the end of the 1980s now looked foolishly optimistic. The oil crisis led to Japan reporting negative growth for 1974. Tanaka's own schemes for remodelling the Japanese archipelago gained considerable popular attention but were wrecked by the fuel crisis and land speculation. The prime minister, who had capitalized on a China boom by recognizing the Peking government shortly after Nixon had visited the people's Republic of China, saw his popularity slump. In December 1974 Tanaka was obliged to resign over financial improprieties and was later arraigned on charges that a decade later are still before the courts. His supporters continue to claim that he is innocent of moves to persuade Japanese corporations to purchase American aircraft. It is also widely rumoured that it was his political rivals that fed possibly incriminating information to journalists who then wrote Japan's version of Watergate. Disgraced or not, Tanaka remains central to Japanese politics. He, too, has no intention of falling on his sword.

Tanaka was replaced by Miki Takeo, a compromise candidate who had served 37 years in the Diet before gaining the premiership. Miki, for all his integrity, was only the leader of a small faction and dependent on the favour of others. His 'Mr Clean' image was exploited by the LDP. He was then dumped. Fukuda replaced Miki, only to find that his reward for improving Japan's economy was the loss of his job to Ohira Masayoshi. Ohira died in the midst of general election campaign in 1980 – somewhat conveniently it has to be said for the LDP. His dissolution of the lower house of the Diet, when faced with intraparty difficulties and scandals, appeared to leave the LDP at risk. Opposition parties had expected to fare well in the June election but Ohira's death produced a landslide victory for the government. Confounding predictions of future coalition rule, the conservatives, under another compromise leader, this time the loyal party stalwart Suzuki Zenko, ended up with an absolute majority. Suzuki was, however, rarely comfortable in his post and appeared to be relieved to resign in 1982. The LDP then elected Nakasone Yasuhiro to the premiership. It was a position to which the new leader had long aspired. From the outset he intended to use his office as a pulpit and lead rather than follow public opinion. His attempts to gain understanding for a shift in Japan's foreign policies will be examined elsewhere. In domestic affairs Nakasone faces the potentially embarrassing situation of relying heavily on Tanaka Kakuei's support. No democratic leader likes to be seen to be close to a former prime minister facing severe legal battles which may result in a lengthy gaol sentence.

Historians are often taken to task for admiring only the victors. But, whatever one's opinions of the programmes and methods of the LDP, it is necessary to concentrate on the conservatives to gain a basic picture of present-day Japanese politics. How is it that the party remains so firmly entrenched in office? What of the future? Our answers will be based on an examination of the LDP and its reflection of certain Japanese values and behaviour.

The LDP might be defined as a loose coalition of conservative groups prepared to swallow considerable personal and ideological differences in order to gain and retain office. The composition of the various factions which make up the party has, of course, changed over the years. The roots of the party, as we saw earlier, can be traced back to prewar politics. For our purposes, however, the Yoshida years may provide a useful starting point. Yoshida inevitably built up a sizeable group of followers during his long reign. His supporters tended to be ex-bureaucrats rather than professional politicians, who found shelter under Hatoyama. The struggle continues between descendants of these factions and a whole variety of newer groups. Membership of a strong faction is virtually a *sine qua non* for any ambitious politician, since the faction leaders alone can provide some of the very substantial funds required to win elections. The larger the faction, the greater its political clout with the LDP and consequent influence on the division of the spoils. The party president (by definition also prime minister) attempts to juggle his appointments to cabinet to satisfy his own faction and placate rival contenders. Factionalism is a fact of political life in Japan which is often denounced – even on occasion by politicians – but rarely are steps taken to reduce its pervasiveness. Loyalty to factional leaders cements the groups together at the risk of antagonizing opposing factions. The infighting is sometimes venomous.

Few politicians of any hue could face the future without the aid of factions. Fewer still would be able to gain re-election without the assistance of personal support groups (*koenkai*). Most aspirants carefully cultivate their constituencies through both factional and support groups, since the expense involved in capturing and then retaining a Diet seat is vast. Some politicians now look on this expenditure as an investment which ought, if possible, to be passed on later to their sons or male relatives. Political costs are probably unquantifiable but estimates of upwards of ¥1000,000,000 have been suggested for victorious candidates in the 1983 election. The ability of the LDP at least to assist most of its candidates undoubtedly gives it an edge over all rival parties. The conservatives are able to raise funds through their financial and industrial backers. One common practice is to stage a party in an appropriate hotel and then sell 'tickets' to business firms who are expected to appear *en masse*. Opposition parties employ similar devices where possible but are clearly limited in the amount of support they can expect to enjoy from industry. Alternative schemes are to concentrate on party membership drives (Komei Party) and sales from newspapers (the Japanese Communist Party).

The LDP undoubtedly retains a strong advantage over fund raising. Another important reason for its political good fortune is the gross malapportionment of parliamentary seats. Rural constituencies (heavily LDP in sympathy) have fewer voters than many of the metropolitan areas. Gerrymandering on this scale can hardly be defended. Needless to say, the conservatives have done little to alter this state of affairs. The Supreme Court decided in 1983 to reject opposition charges that elections held under a system whereby the number of voters per seat in the urban Kanagawa prefecture was over five times that of the southern prefecture of Tottori was sufficient reason for declaring the contest void. So long as the courts keep out of this controversial area the LDP possesses a built-in advantage which it will jealously preserve at all costs.

If, as has been frequently claimed by political observers, factions 'are the focus of Japanese politics', what remains to be said of the central party organizations of the LDP? The party, like the prime minister, is often weak. Initiatives rarely come from party headquarters. The premier's men usually pack the senior posts but have to pay some regard to the voices from rival factions. Yet after a shift to electing the party president by party members as well as LDP Dietmen was revised, the party's officials have re-emerged with greater power. Their influence over deciding which candidates will receive official party backing is an important weapon, as is the secretary general's discretion over government appointments. The absurd frequency with which cabinets are made and then reconstructed plays into the hands of those LDP officials who, in consultation with the prime minister, ultimately shuffle the names and decide the new government. Senior political figures can expect, therefore, to hold a wide variety of posts during their careers. Whether they have the time or inclination to master the details of office is a moot point.

Finally, to turn to issues which readers may have thought ought to have been raised earlier. Ideology is not a particularly important issue in LDP affairs. Party manifestos are vague (even by Japanese standards) and stress bromides such as the need to develop further Japan's relations with the United States and promote economic policies to secure the people's livelihood. The share of the electorate that votes for the LDP does so on more personal grounds. Politicians (normally drawn from the local prefecture) are supported because they and their relatives have secure personal ties with the neighbourhood and can be relied on to promote the constituency in Tokyo. It is not the party but the Dietman who is the centre of attention. It is his support groups that have enabled him to gain the votes for victory. It is he who has paid the bill for the lunchboxes and seen to it that more tangible rewards are forthcoming when the election is in doubt.

The LDP's future is not yet in question. Money, out of date electoral boundaries, gratitude built up over the many years in office and the state of the opposition have all made their contribution to this state of affairs. Much of the electorate appears to be sufficiently satisfied with the status quo continually to renew the party's mandate. It wins rural and semi-rural seats with ease and sufficient urban votes to be able to see off charges that it is merely the party of the countryside. Since the rural population has declined precipitately since the war it could not, even with the aid of gerrymandered constituencies, retain power through its agricultural following. It wins because it organizes better and has demonstrated to many Japanese that it can still govern. Some negative factors also work in the conservatives favour. There is undoubtedly an element of 'better the devil you know' behind parts of the LDP's vote.

The opposition parties share little in common beyond a belief that the LDP has overstayed its welcome and deserves to take a respite from the burdens of office. The electorate, however, has considerable difficulty in envisaging any of the many possible opposition party coalitions which could eventually replace the conservatives. (No one opposition party is sufficiently strong to be able to consider rule by itself.) Since power has largely eluded the opposition our account will necessarily be brief. Victors' justice is invariably harsh on perennial losers.

The largest opposition party and the one which deserves the most attention is the Japan Socialist Party (JSP). In some ways it was the mirror image of the LDP. It used to be an overwhelmingly urban party and has a strong ideological foundation. Yet, like the conservatives, its position too is under threat. It fears the loss of its traditional metropolitan vote to newer parties and has had to suffer damaging publicity over factional splits. The JSP has also had its differences with its traditional paymasters. The trades unions are divided now over the advantages to be gained by supporting the Socialists. While the largest labour federation (Sohyo) encourages the Socialists, there are important rivals that take a less radical stance. The second most powerful labour grouping (Domei) helps finance the more moderate Democratic Socialist Party (DSP). Questions over funding and the gradual decline of the share of the non-LDP vote going to the JSP have sapped some of the confidence remaining within the party. It has enemies on all sides and major internal feudings to resolve. There have been recent attempts to modify the JSP's stance on security and defence matters in order to prepare the ground with other opposition groups for coalition discussions but such moves may well alienate the left-wing of the party. Public opinion has probably shifted further and faster than the JSP can easily accommodate on issues such as the US–Japan Security Treaty. The JSP elected Ishibashi Masashi as its new chairman in September 1983 in the hope that he might be able to reconsider the party's labour ties and play down the 'unarmed neutrality' plank in the party programme. One academic with links to the party has noted, however, that 'what the JSP needs is not only a new head, but a new body and feet as well'.

The Socialists are not alone in facing present and future difficulties. Those who a few years ago had been confidently predicting some form of opposition alliance to replace the LDP have by the mid 1980s to account for the failure of such hopes. It is not only the JSP that has disappointed its supporters. The smaller opposition parties have also to reckon with their dashed dreams.

The Japan Communist Party (JCP) and Komeito (Clean Government Party) are the two groups to the left and right of the Socialists. The JCP has strong individual membership (a rare virtue in Japanese politics where party subscriptions are frequently paid by politicians out of their own pockets) and possesses adequate financial backing. It has not, however, been able to make a substantial breakthrough into political respectability. It has won some metropolitan seats and has a determined chairman in Miyamoto Kenji, but it is unlikely to be a popular choice in any possible anti-LDP coalition. As Komeito is its sworn enemy, it is difficult to imagine the JCP and the political arm of a staunchly Buddhist movement joining hands. Both parties tend to chase urban workers who feel neglected by the LDP. Political commentators have suggested that both the JCP and Komeito may have reached the demographic limits of their appeal. The Democratic Socialist Party (a breakaway JSP group) is closer ideologically to Komeito and displays a very different foreign policy posture from that of the JCP. The DSP can have slim hopes of a share in power unless the LDP loses still more parliamentary seats.

For the opposition parties all eyes remain focused on the LDP. Its apparent stability amidst unfavourable international economic conditions has blunted the anti-conservative trends of a decade ago. The left has been obliged gradually to retreat over foreign policy issues as the public mood has concentrated on domestic affairs as times have got relatively harder. The growing number of floating voters and the speed with which many ex-students have jettisoned past ideological baggage once they take on family and professional responsibilities is hardly encouraging to the left's party organizers. (One exception to this shift may be the widespread distrust of Japan's nuclear energy programme. Critics of nuclear power have capitalized on Japan's 'nuclear allergy', while its defenders have seen the opposition as more accurately based on 'nuclear ideology'.) The anger behind the street demonstrations of the 1960s, when Tokyo was brought to a halt over the security treaty and university issues, was already fading by 1970; Prime Minister Sato was able to extend the security treaty without the turmoil that had led to his predecessor's downfall.

The LDP's revival has undoubtedly been aided by the government's successful anti-inflation campaigns and the perceived prosperity of most Japanese (rightly or wrongly 90% of those polled regard themselves as middle-class). A nation of 'haves' is seemingly reluctant to jeopardize its gains by voting for new faces and inexperienced office holders. The factory worker nearing retirement and the white-collar employee (salaryman) who can barely keep up with his mortgage repayments may often feel neglected by the LDP but the opposition parties do not always offer a safer haven. The inability of the opposition parties to capture substantial votes from the LDP to enlarge their respective national followings – never mind at the local level where the conservatives' strength can hardly be challenged – leaves the status quo intact. For the present, the party of the establishment stays put. Those betting on major change in Japanese politics deserve long odds.

The LDP forms one leg of the tripod that determines Japan's destiny.

It has, however, two most powerful partners and rivals in the central bureaucracy and Japanese industry. When all three agents are pulling in the same direction the result is indeed a formidable spectacle. This does not, of course, occur on all occasions and the co-operation between the three may be exaggerated. 'Japan Inc.' can be a misleading caption. The idea of an unholy alliance of Japanese politicians, civil servants and business leaders plotting to pick off yet another European or North American industrial sector ought to be treated with some scepticism.

Yet the importance of the decisions of Japan's bureaucrats over national goals is not in question. This is no new phenomenon. It has, though, been aided by the collapse of court and military influence on policy making. The number of Japanese élites has clearly declined since the ending of the Pacific war and the status of the bureaucracy (hardly insignificant during the Meiji period) has been enhanced. The same cannot be maintained for Japanese politicians who are treated with far less respect. This continuation of prewar attitudes towards Dietmen and bureaucrats is not about to change. Public cynicism and even open hostility in parts of the electorate with regard to political figures benefits the civil service. Its senior officials have indeed felt that they are entitled to make public policy. They often do, but some might question whether this is entirely admirable. (European readers may detect certain parallels between the situation in Japan and the administrative and decision-making processes nearer home. 'Yes Minister' – a British comedy series on the ability of bureaucrats to control their nominal masters – is not merely a British problem.)

The civil service was subject to reform during the Allied occupation of Japan. But, as with a number of other attempts at altering Japanese institutions, the changes did not entirely succeed. This was probably inevitable. SCAP had little choice but to employ Japan's bureaucracy in its efforts to promote reform and could hardly avoid turning a blind eye to the civil service's footdragging, since it badly needed administrative co-operation. Alterations to the structure of the central bureaucracy through the National Civil Service Law in 1947 did reduce the arbitrary nature of its power but public attitudes and the competitive recruitment system have engendered an outlook 'more of pride of place and sense of executive mission than of consciousness of service to the people'.

The administration of the civil service is in the hands of the National Personnel Authority which reports to the prime minister. Bureaucrats do not have the right to strike. Their impartiality is generally assumed, though the frequent instances of senior officials leaving to join private industry, public corporations and parliament have led to public unease. This all too easily creates the impression of collusion between the bureaucracy and conservative forces in the country. (This too is a familiar feature. Ties between the Meiji government and infant industries were particularly close. Without state intervention and financial assistance Japanese capitalism might have found it impossible to compete against Western industrial and financial expertise.) The press reports in detail the transfer of bureaucrats to second careers in the private sector, yet 'parachuting' continues. If the phrase 'creative conservatism' – to take the subtitle of a recent account of Japanese policy studies – implies a widespread public and private liaison, then it is doubtful whether these links can always be defended.

Japan's bureaucrats, despite one's reservations on the boundaries of their influence, deserve a major share in any praise for Japan's current domestic and international position. The price may be a self-perpetuating élite (often drawn from the law faculty of Tokyo University), but the graphic contrast between the Japan of the immediate post-war years and the consumerism of today speaks for itself. No economy could have expanded tenfold between 1950 and 1980 without an efficient, capable civil service. How were the bureaucrats able to get Japan moving after the war? How have they continued to guide the Japanese economy through the high growth years and beyond?

We ought first to look at the structure of the civil service and then explore how it determines economic policy. By international standards Japan's bureaucracy is not large, nor is its structure geared to recruiting entrants from a wide variety of universities. It is rare indeed to encounter women graduates from provincial universities on the career escalator. As in other nations, the ministries involved with national finance have been generally regarded as the more prestigious and thereby the likely home of the abler recruits. The Ministry of Finance (MOF) and the Ministry of International Trade and Industry (MITI) are the twin pinnacles of power. The limited prospect of transfer outside one's initial ministry further intensifies an already strong sense of loyalty. The consequences are often a healthy *élan* and a less constructive rivalry with competing ministries and agencies. Most ministries are situated within easy walking distance of each other in the Kasumigaseki district of Tokyo, but the psychological barriers can be considerable.

MITI is the ministry best known outside Japan. Foreign journalists enjoy depicting it as 'the maestro that orchestrates Japanese industrial policy', while academics often develop the contradictory theme that

MITI is a fading power. The reality may depend on one's historical perspective. MITI's role has undoubtedly changed with the progress of the Japanese economy from austerity to affluence. Its success in leading industrial recovery has necessarily altered its current functions. Techniques which were appropriate in the 1950s and early 1960s to generate growth are inapplicable now under changed international circumstances. Where does MITI stand today? Will it be possible for the ministry to retain the bulk of its past influence?

To start with the obvious. The Japanese economy is neither a fully fledged free-enterprise system (what nation is when the rhetoric is removed?) nor a centrally planned model. MITI thrives less on direct command than indirect suggestion and veiled threat. A young graduate in his first years at MITI quickly discovers the pleasures of telephoning senior company executives to offer tentative proposals on possible changes in industrial policy. The joys of 'administrative guidance' can be sweet indeed. By a succession of hints and occasional losses of temper MITI has often got its own way. This need be no cause for surprise if one accepts that 'Japanese enterprises have been used to extensive protection by the state and have tended to apply for special relief measures or to resort to cartel-like arrangements in times of trouble'. The market mechanism is far from a sacred cow. The government is expected to intervene to press for structural change. MITI's particular concerns involve the encouragement of new industries (micro-electronics, biotechnology, and new generation computers) and the rationalization of declining sectors (textiles is one of its perennial headaches).

Commentators are generally agreed that MITI's word is no longer the law it was a generation ago. Some of the industries that received earlier support have repaid the ministry by disregarding its more recent solicitations. Perhaps this should be welcomed as evidence that the ministry does not have all the answers and cannot always enforce its will on recalcitrant industries. Yet by most standards MITI has made a major contribution to the shape of contemporary Japan. Its industrial policy has generally been followed. The role of the state in setting economic goals and then encouraging particular industries to conform to its guidelines has paid handsome dividends. It may be some rough measure of MITI's achievements that American voices have increasingly called for the creation of an equivalent body in Washington.

In budgetary terms and in political influence MOF stands higher than MITI. Kishi Nobusuke has been the only vice-minister of MITI or its forerunner (the Ministry of Commerce and Industry) to gain the premiership, in contrast to the MOF backgrounds of prime ministers Ikeda and Fukuda. But MITI takes pride of place in our account because of its efforts to create a capital-intensive economy out of the ashes of postwar Japan. MOF's task is to work through its fiscal and monetary controls to operate the Japanese economy. It prepares the national budget, negotiates at a lengthy and arduous series of ministerial conferences over the size of each department's expenditures, and is responsible for administrating the budget after it has been approved by the Diet.

MOF's difficulties today are compounded by the growing size (and therefore political importance) of the nation's budget deficit. The government and public opinion are fully aware of the haemorrhaging caused by public corporations and nationalized industries (Japan National Railways is a national joke), as well as the agricultural support programmes. The pressure to rectify the seemingly endless rise in the deficit and the need to continue to float government bonds to cover the gap is strong. So too is the counter-pressure to preserve the status-quo. Bureaucrats have no wish to amalgamate rival bureaus, unionists dislike the surrender of their privileges and politicians fear the inevitable backlash from those who lose their perquisites. Administrative reform of Japanese government finances is certain to be a hard road and its eventual fate far from assured.

There remain two important ministries that deserve mention because of their political influence. The activities of both the Ministry of Agriculture and Forestry and the Ministry of Construction are carefully watched by conservative politicians, since agriculture subsidies and public works projects form the basis of Japan's pork-barrel politics. Developments of social facilities and the price at which the government purchases farm produce are key issues to numerous LDP Dietmen. No politician is likely to get ahead without assistance from bureaucrats in these ministries. Those in MITI, for example, who would wish to liberalize agriculture in order to deflect foreign criticism of Japan's trade policies, face endless disappointment. The government can only go so far if it wants to retain office. Agriculture, however expensive it may prove to the Japanese consumer, is seemingly inviolable. It may be cheaper to import rice, beef and oranges but there are limits to the extent of liberalization that can be expected. Likewise, the few Japanese tobacco growers can rest assured that their interests will weigh heavily with the Minister of Agriculture and the LDP. Much of this can be infuriating to farmers' organizations in the United States and elsewhere.

The United States administration demonstrated its dissatisfaction by filing a complaint against Japan under GATT regulations in the summer of 1983, but open markets would destroy Japanese beef and citrus farmers and have immediate and far reaching repercussions for the LDP. Japan will presumably continue to make gradual concessions, while resisting any major change in its protectionist attitudes. Political realities will hinder foreign attempts to further penetrate Japanese agricultural markets.

Japanese industry forms the final segment of our analysis. Its contribution to the political process is far less public than the legislative–executive arm and probably less influential than the Japanese bureaucracy. It prefers usually to stay in the background, no doubt in order to dampen public memories of its role as paymaster to the parties in the 1920s and 1930s. What does business get out of its involvement in the political arena? Is it content with the system?

The answer varies with which area of business one examines. The immense variety of scale within the Japanese economy makes generalization risky. Some issues though are reasonably clear. Big business is an important, if declining, fund-raiser for the conservatives. Medium- and small-scale industries and services contribute far less money but probably play a larger role at the grass-roots level. This is explained by the standing such enterprises often possess in the local communities, which can be translated into political influence. Small shopkeepers and family businesses are staunch supporters of the LDP. They expect the party, for its share of the bargain, to take note of their special interests. The conservatives, for example, have devised legislation to prevent encroachment by supermarket chains which would otherwise decimate the corner shop. Likewise, family firms can easily gain access to soft loans to improve their facilities. Small wonder that voter turnout in such groups remains impressively high and virtually unanimous in its political allegiance. Clearly these small firms need the government as much as, if not more than, the LDP needs them. The numerous small shopkeepers and backstreet factories employing a handful of workers represent the less efficient elements in Japan's complicated distribution and subcontracting systems. Such elements were until recently the backbone of the LDP. The party may be altering but they have nowhere to go.

Big business has at least four powerful umbrella organizations to ensure that its voice is heard loud and clear in LDP circles. The best known is the Federation of Economic Organizations (Keidanren). Although it is not always in agreement with the other large business groups, it retains considerable prestige and is often assumed to speak for industry. Its chairman is expected to have public views on who ought to be the next LDP president and will give advice to the government on what it sees as correct economic policy for the nation. What business is assumed to want above all else from the LDP is continuity; it welcomes assurances and evidence that the party is not about to fragment. It wants no move to the left. Like any pressure group, it seeks to hold the conservatives to their promises over tax concessions, generous assistance when whole industries fall on hard times and an economic climate that continues to respect growth. Industrial circles have done well out of the arrangement.

Opposition to the LDP comes from many quarters. The first, as we have seen, is contained within the party itself. Other political groupings also form an obvious countervailing force to conservative rule. Their lack of success, however, in toppling the LDP has exposed all too painfully their limitations. Newspapers are now widely regarded as providing an alternative voice capable on occasion of standing up to the LDP. The Japanese appetite for news is vast. Impressive literacy figures and lengthy commuting periods, if not always sufficient elbow room, combine to saturate the nation with newsprint. The largest daily, *Yomiuri Shimbun*, had a morning circulation in 1981 of 8.58 million copies. Its nearest rival, *Asahi Shimbun*, was hot on its heels with sales of nearly 7.5 million. These figures suggest, at the very least, potential power. The drawback, however, is the tendency for most of the press to speak with one voice most of the time. It is generally the case that 'all the newspapers look and sound the same'. The reluctance to discuss Mr Tanaka's financial improprieties and an unwillingness to upset the Chinese government before permission had been granted for the major newspapers to station correspondents in Peking are examples of not wishing to go out on a limb. This conformity compounds other problems. Since journalistic coverage of foreign affairs is not likely to change many existing views of the world, some would claim that an opportunity to widen popular perceptions is being missed. Given the influence and immense resources of the Japanese press, this is unfortunate. Yet in comparison with the blatant 'show biz' approach of most British newspapers the Japanese press has much to be proud of.

The public is unlikely to gain any improved image of international affairs from watching television, the newspapers' insipid rival. Practically continuous commercial television on a host of channels offers a mediocre diet. Sunday programmes run to a set formula of quiz shows, golf and baseball, singing competitions and soap operas. The emphasis is obviously on entertainment. Neither the tired commuter nor television sponsors want anything too strenuous. Such strictures apply to a lesser degree to Japan's public broadcasting organization, NHK (Nippon Hoso Kyokai, Japan Broadcasting Corporation). NHK is financed by monthly fees. The standards it sets itself are high, but it too has to compete with the commercial stations for mass audiences. Still, NHK remains a notable Japanese institution with two television channels (one entirely educational), three radio networks and an overseas broadcasting service (Radio Japan). It is not an arm of the Japanese government and is most unlikely to surrender its editorial autonomy.

Japanese pressure groups share three targets. All aim to create a favourable public image, to garner the support of sufficient numbers of Dietmen and, above all, to persuade the higher bureaucracy of the justice and urgency of their cause. The last is crucial since it is often the attitude of the civil service that determines the fate of intended legislation. Little moves without its nod. Two important and frequently cited examples of successful pressure groups are the business associations and trades unions. The LDP's ties with industry have become sufficiently organized for commentators to describe the relationship as 'symbiotic'. Likewise, the railway, postal and teachers' unions have developed very close links with the JSP. Unionists fill their seats in the Diet in much the same way that businessmen and ex-bureaucrats pack the LDP's parliamentary ranks. Such trends are likely to continue as the already astronomical costs of fighting an election (particularly for the conservatives) increase still further. Detailed research on constituency issues, greater stress on personalizing each candidate and lower voter turnouts ensure that the search for funds is never-ending. Business groups and unions will remain the staple supporters of the LDP and JSP.

Yet the pressure group *par excellence* has to be the Agricultural Co-operatives Association (Nokyo). It can seemingly organize a mass demonstration in Kasumigaseki at the drop of a hat. It produces apparently compelling arguments why a small, vulnerable, resource-poor nation like Japan should attempt to be self-sufficient in agricultural produce. Its voice is not to be ignored since almost all farmers belong to one of its chapters. The LDP would very much prefer to dispense with the quite anomalous rice-support system and has recently shown a certain willingness to face the anger of the co-operatives and hold down the price of rice to merely token 1% increases. This takes courage since Nokyo and the opposition parties could combine to present a formidable challenge. The long-term solution to excessive rice production from small uneconomical farmers (the producer price of rice is approximately four to five times world prices) would presumably require both consolidation of paddyfields and greater crop diversification. Demography at least is on the side of change but political resistance from agricultural interests is assured.

Citizens' movements (*shimin undo*) have been hailed as a harbinger of Japan's political maturity. Their supporters insist that such *ad hoc* coalitions mark a decisive step away from rural deference to urban assertiveness. By 1983, however, the enthusiasm that marked their inception in the 1960s and early 1970s had waned and it was less apparent whether these newer pressure groups would be able to sustain themselves. What are citizens' movements? Why did they receive such a favourable press a decade ago?

A loose definition of a citizens' movement might be a single-issue coalition, often with an ideological bias, intent on exposing local grievances. The groups which have received the most publicity have been engaged in fighting legal battles to gain compensation for industrial pollution. The most notorious struggle – and the one to become a brief household name in the West – was the Minamata case. Responsibility for the high incidence of organic mercury found in fish of Kyushu was finally proved after the corporation involved and its employees had long denied it was at fault. A series of lengthy cases elsewhere led the LDP to tighten up anti-pollution regulations. The results are apparent in tough car exhaust laws which have generally reduced the incidence of smog in metropolitan areas. Other environmentalist groups have attempted to prevent the construction of high-rise buildings which left the surrounding households bereft of sunlight, and campaigned against the noise levels caused by superexpress trains and night flying at some airports. Other citizens' movements have demonstrated against nuclear power, in favour of a freedom of information act (badly needed in a bureaucratic society such as Japan) and supported changes in the nationality laws.

The advocates of citizens' movements see such action committees as a new and virtuous form of participatory politics. The campaigns selected tend to be anti-capitalist and anti-Town Hall. The degree of their success in attacking what was then a low public concern over polluted rivers and urban air has left the movements with fewer adversaries. The reduction in economic opportunities has also taken its toll of potential supporters, who may be more concerned with their standard of living than abstract rhetoric on the quality of life.

Protest movements have also influenced local government by short-circuiting elected assemblies. The trend has been for citizens' groups to deal directly with administrative officials. (Chief executives in Japanese local and prefectural government are elected.) The occupation had attempted to create greater local autonomy and encourage decentralization as a barrier to the prewar position where the Home Ministry had appointed its nominees to local and regional posts. The situation since has been to alter parts of the 1947 reforms and to gradually take back some of the powers previously granted to the localities. Matters concerning policing, finance and education up to senior high school are still partly the responsibility of local government. Most local assemblymen, mayors and governors either stand with the support of the conservatives or claim to be inedpendents, usually with moderate leanings. The time when 'red' Kyoto, Tokyo and Osaka all had left-wing governors is over. Local government is now more closely tied to national voting, with many citizens adopting the view that an LDP mayor will be better able to curry favours for his locality when he makes his frequent visits to Tokyo.

Local government is increasingly subject to adverse criticism. Gone for good are the days when local authorities could do no wrong. Press stories of lax time-keeping, enormous pensions and timid management have hurt, particularly as the public is sensitive to any rumour of tax increases. Well-furnished ward offices and newly opened cultural centres provide a monument to the pre-Oil-Shock era when regionalism and welfare seemed to have a future. The picture has since changed, though municipal bodies have been slow to recognize how out of date their thinking is in danger of becoming. Local government will have to be persuaded to sweat off its surplus fat if the government's finances are to be corrected. It has fewer allies than it once imagined it had.

In order to demonstrate its political maturity and to speed up the ending of Western extra-territoriality that had permitted foreigners in the treaty ports to be tried in their own consular courts, the Meiji leaders had first introduced codified law in the 1880s. The Japanese legal system has since undergone considerable change and is now an amalgam of French and German civil law and later Anglo-Saxon revisions. Japanese law today rests on the postwar constitution. Under it the judiciary possesses complete judicial power without interference from the executive branch, in the same way that legislative power is the exclusive domain of the Diet and executive responsibility belongs to the cabinet. There has been no return to the 1930s when government was 'policeman, prosecutor and judge'. The Justice Ministry organizes the hierarchy of courts and their procurators but investigations are conducted by the police under the National Public Safety Commission.

The independence of the courts was intended to be further protected by the Supreme Court's right to judicial review. This gave the judiciary the right to determine the constitutionality of all legislation. The Supreme Court, however, has been very reluctant to use this power, since it prefers to see popular sovereignty as resting on the legislative branch of government and wishes to maintain amicable relations with the Diet to prevent any repetition of prewar executive encroachment on to legal terrain. The courts have not wished, for example, to get involved in political controversy. Rightly or wrongly, the Supreme Court ruled that it was not for it to determine whether the US–Japan Security Treaty was illegal (Sunakawa Case, 1959). It has also, as we have seen, avoided getting snared on electoral boundary reform issues, preferring to leave such matters to the Diet. The contrast with the activism of the American Supreme Court is decidedly marked.

The Japanese courts have been less hesitant over interpretations of constitutional rights. The constitution provides (in articles 10–40, Rights and Duties of the People) for an extensive list of individual rights, though these are qualified by 'public welfare' considerations (articles 12 and 13). Civil rights include the separation of religion and state (an issue that still gives rise to fears from Buddhists and Christians that the government favours Shintoism) and academic freedom. The constitution also provided in its lengthy category of human rights for sexual equality, mobility of labour, collective bargaining and detailed legal treatment including habeas corpus. Much that was alien in 1947 to many Japanese, particularly with regard to family structure, is now accepted as commonplace.

Yet generational and political attitudes continue to play their part in public receptivity to the constitution. The fact that this American-inspired document has survived without change for 35 years is not in itself proof of its popularity. There remain some LDP voices, including that of the present prime minister, who would wish to revise the constitution. Dispute centres, of course, on article 9. The left insists that the 'peace constitution' ought to be protected since it persists in fearing that any alteration would only be for expansionist ends. The LDP at various times since 1952 has pointed out the anomalies of squaring Japan's military (euphemistically known as the Self-Defence Forces) with a constitution which, to the non-legal mind at least, appears to 'renounce war as a sovereign right of the nation and the threat or use of force as a means of settling international disputes'. The revisionists are most unlikely at present to get their way within the LDP, let alone the nation at large (article 96 deals with amendments to the constitution), but the issue is unlikely to disappear entirely. The return of a strengthened LDP majority and shifts in the international situation might make revision once again a possibility. Until then the government and people will have to continue to believe that the maintenance of its army, navy and air forces are in accordance with a constitution which is decidedly pacifist.

The Japanese legal system gives us some pointers to the nation's social patterns. The courts and their officials are held in high repute. The Chief Judge of the Supreme Court is selected by the cabinet and appointed by the Emperor. His salary is on a par with that of the prime minister. The other members of his bench are subject to popular review by the electorate but the fact that none of them has ever been recalled is evidence again of the status they appear to enjoy. Among the inferior courts the one most likely to involve the public is the Family Court, which has the difficult task of adjudicating domestic issues such as inheritance and, increasingly, divorce.

Yet resort to law remains a rare occurrence for the Japanese people, who prefer to reach a solution (of sorts) outside the legal system. Paradoxically, perhaps, the public both respects and avoids the law. It dislikes litigation, but readily swallows what Europeans might well find an irksome amount of bureaucratic command. Frequent procession to the local ward office for copies of family registers, permits for parking, and notice of change of address is accepted fatalistically. So too is the haughty attitude of officialdom towards the public it ought to be serving. Legalism rules. It is safest to assume the bureaucrat knows best, even when he does not.

3

Economic growth and consolidation

The world is looking eastward. Reportage on Japan's economy is rarely out of the headlines. Its products are on the roads and in the shops from Perth to Portland. How did Japan do it? Is there some special Japanese ingredient for economic success? Or can other nations also follow its path to modernization and industrialization? Both advanced and developing nations wish to know. The subject is strewn with rival theories and erudite tomes. We shall diffidently attempt to describe the central features of the Japanese economy and then offer an historical explanation of how it has attained its present position.

The economic system in Japan is a mixture of free market competition and strong state intervention. One ministry defined this as a 'plan-orientated market economy', though entrepreneurs instantly reject such labels and point to the fierce in-fighting which undoubtedly does take place in some sectors. It would appear, however, that the role of the Japanese bureaucracy is one fundamental factor observable in any dissection of the economy. Its influence is substantial. Its prestige, political skills and policy-making power allow senior civil servants virtually to dominate national economic counsels. (We have referred earlier to the handicaps many ministers have to work under.) MITI has played an important part in encouraging the development of new industries, the consolidation of others and the cartelization of those judged to be terminal cases if left to market forces. Naturally it has had to face strong opposition to its recommendations from industrialists and rival bureaucracies, such as the Fair Trade Commission.

What is noteworthy is not that MITI has made mistakes (its wish to reduce the number of Japanese car manufacturers is continually brought up to illustrate its fallibility), but that there have been relatively few major ones. It could not, of course, have its way on every occasion and its heyday was the 1950s when industry was more amenable to its suggestions. Yet even today MITI's influence is hard to avoid. New generation computer manufacturers and ailing aluminium smelting companies alike receive assistance from its officials. Key industries from the past usually get a decent burial from the ministry that sponsored their growth a generation earlier. Import restrictions, low-interest loans from government financial institutions, investment co-ordination and merger schemes are all part of MITI's repertoire. Japan has thus evolved a complicated series of state–private-industry relationships that work. They do not succeed all the time, but the results compare very favourably with those of any other mixed economy. But Japan's Industrial Policy – the phrase is enjoying a degree of notoriety in the United States – would never have received its current attention if its bureaucrats had not first obtained the co-operation of industry, the financial community and labour. The best bureaucrats would have achieved little without the managerial and technical skills of Japanese enterprises. We shall turn to them next.

Japanese industry shares with Japan's Industrial Policy the brunt of foreign criticism of things Japanese. Criticism has expanded in direct proportion to Japan's increasing success. Understanding has advanced at a slower pace and has frequently been submerged under a barrage of harsh editorials, parliamentary questions and congressional testimony. Popular images in the West are disturbingly simplistic. Japanese factories apparently all commence with the entire workforce in identical grey fatigues chanting the company song and doing mass press-ups. This is followed by an intolerably long workday, punctuated only by intervals to attend Quality Control circles, the workforce spurning all tea breaks.

Most foreign interest has been directed to the large Japanese manufacturing companies. These form the relatively small number of important exporters in steel, cars, machine tools and electrical goods that have made consumers throughout the world aware of Japanese products. The high proportion of heavy and chemical industries in industrial production is clearly the consequence of government influence on Japanese investment patterns since the 1950s. Successor industries are, as we have seen, continually subject to the same planning procedures and scrutiny that launched Japan's postwar industrialization programme. It is to be expected that those that can demonstrate winning potential will again receive administrative assistance and that the less successful will be given little of the British-style 'lame duck' treatment. Losers are consigned to the scrap heap.

To identify the companies that make the news may now be in order.

Japan's largest firms include two car manufacturers (Toyota and Nissan), Matsushita Electric, Hitachi, Nippon Steel (formed by the merger of Fuji and Yawata) and Mitsubishi Heavy Industries. All are giant operations by world standards. All existed, often in very different circumstances, before the Pacific war. All are beholden to certain banks for favourable opportunities to raise capital, and some were part of Zaibatsu groupings before 1945. Employees in such firms have a range of benefits unknown to less fortunate workers in smaller enterprises. The Western view of Japanese industry is drawn from these major corporations, with their 'lifetime' employment practices, promotion largely dependent on seniority and company-based unions. Large firms (defined as those employing more than 1,000 people) are in a strong position to hire the best graduates and thereby perpetuate their dominance. Once taken on, new recruits can expect lengthy periods of in-company training and future attendance at refresher courses. White-collar workers usually remain with their company, or one of its subsidiaries, until retirement.

It is noteworthy that our list does not include any representatives from either the textile or shipbuilding industries. Such companies were once world-beaters but, although still important to the fate of many local communities, are now in decline. Textiles had been the vanguard of Japan's prewar industrialization but by 1971 accounted for only 10% of total manufacturing employment and now contribute less than 5% of Japan's exports. Shipbuilding is following down the same path as it encounters increased competition from countries such as South Korea and Brazil.

Most of Japanese industry is neither large nor particularly interested in exporting. Small enterprises concentrating on the domestic market form the backbone of the economy. They offer lower wages, far fewer fringe benefits and have less of the security associated with employment in blue-riband companies. The dualism of the Japanese economy, prevalent before the war, persists today. It was a product of a large surplus agrarian population (usually excluding the eldest sons, who were expected both to manage the family smallholding and look after their parents) that came to the cities looking for work. The result was depressed wages and low productivity levels. Since the exodus of the 1950s and early 1960s the wage differential has been reduced considerably but is unlikely to be ironed out, given the present economic climate.

In comparison with the United States, West Germany and Britain there can be little doubt that the structure of Japanese industry is quite different. Japan is, and will remain, the odd man out. It is a nation of small shopkeepers, family businesses and minuscule subcontractors. Workers on the Toyota assembly line receive a better deal than the subcontracting panel beaters and turners who work for lower wages and risk getting the sack when times are hard. Nearly 60% of the Japanese labour force in 1979 worked in establishments employing 1–99 people. Only 13% are employed now in firms with over 1,000 workers, which is half the American figure and only a third of the West German total.

The dual structure applies to the service sector as well. Japan, like other advanced countries, is already a post-industrial state. The phrase, for our purposes, means no more than that a majority of the workforce is engaged in the tertiary or service sector. In the case of Japan such a position was attained by 1970. In 1981, Bank of Japan statistics indicated that 55% of all employees were then in service industries. We shall look later at the possible social implications of this gradual shift from agriculture to industry and finally to the tertiary stage, but we ought to be wary of those commentators who imagine this may prompt major cultural change. There is nothing particularly modern, for example, about Japan's immensely complicated distribution system. It is both a highly complex and strictly controlled mutual benefit society, which aims to protect a web of manufacturers, wholesalers and retailers. It does this admirably, at the expense of the consumer. Outsiders, both Japanese and foreign, are not welcome.

The situation is more promising in the technological areas of Japan's service sector. Yet it has to be borne in mind that almost 50% of the 30 million workers in the tertiary section are still employed in wholesale and retail businesses. (Japan rarely conforms to Western sociological patterns.) For those engaged in banking, trading companies (immensely important for handling Japan's imports and exports) and information services there would appear to be a brighter future. Technological research by Japan's 700,000 scientists and laboratory staff is designed to equip Japanese industry to face the future with a degree of confidence largely absent in western Europe. Japan does not win many Nobel prizes and has no equivalent of the NASA Apollo programme or the Anglo-French Concorde project, but its introduction of computers and robots on a large scale suggests that it deploys its research for growth purposes. This is hardly surprising since private industry rather than the government usually has to foot the bill.

Interest in contemporary Japan has centred on its substantial economic achievements. The titles employed to account for Japan's progress

– if progress it be – have made it apparent where many authors stand. Those in favour like to attach 'miracle', 'giant' or 'number one' to their books. Severer critics prefer instead to employ 'imperialism today', 'crisis' or 'ugly' as clues to their thinking. There is also a less adventurist third group that eschews all such frivolity and opts for strict neutrality, at least as far as the title page goes. Any questions we pose on the Japanese economy may, of course, reflect our personal prejudices. Still the subject must be tackled head-on. How did Japan make it? What were the costs? What might its future be over the next decade? What consequences could this have for its trading partners?

Japan was down but not out in September 1945. At first glance, however, the situation looked hopeless. The economy was clearly a shambles. The cities were frequently no more than rubble. The rice crop had failed. Repatriation of civilians and soldiers could only impose further strains on hungry families and confused bureaucrats. The Japanese empire had been liquidated. Countless Japanese had lost their homes and jobs. Yet the trams were running almost immediately. Shanty towns sprouted up overnight. Allied journalists saw how quickly the damage was being cleared away. Hunger led to rampant blackmarketeering and hoarding but the people scratched out a living under wretched urban conditions. (The farmers often did very well at the expense of the cities.) Any inventory of companies that today are international names will show how many were founded in the grim days after Japan's surrender. There were opportunities and some made the most of them. The nation – it never thought of itself as anything less even in the humiliation of defeat – had a host of assets which it could continue to draw on as it had during the war. Education, social cohesion and the spur of poverty go some way to explaining Japan's recovery.

The barest of statistics will tell one side of the story. The Pacific war left Japan without a quarter of its national wealth, since factories and shops were gutted, the merchant marine had been sunk and transportation was badly damaged. Industrial output was slow to pick up and attempts to stimulate the economy merely resulted in hyperinflation and low growth. Only by 1952 had industrial production recovered to 15% above 1934–6 levels. The following year, as if to underline Japan's new sovereignty, was the first occasion when national income surpassed its prewar peak.

The occupation forms the first of our five chronological divisions on the postwar Japanese economy. It was obviously an unpleasant period of food shortages, labour unrest and general uncertainty. Not until the 1970s was Japan to witness once again some of the tensions and confusions of an earlier era it thought it had permanently outgrown. Foreign verdicts on the progress of Japan by 1952 were decidedly mixed. John Foster Dulles termed the situation more or less hopeless, while the British textile industry was obsessed with what it saw as a Japanese revival that would kill off Lancashire. France and Australia also adopted a cautious approach to future Japanese trading prospects by joining Britain in resisting United States pleas that Japan be granted Most-Favoured-Nation treatment. All three countries blocked Japan's first application to join GATT. Many Western industrial powers clearly saw the occupation as no more than a breathing space for their own economies. Japan, it was widely assumed, would quickly pick itself up. Its international competitors rarely doubted that a reconstructed Japan, aided by American financial assistance prompted by the Cold War in east Asia, would be back to renew its prewar challenge. Events soon proved such jeremiads accurate.

The Allies' initial attitude to Japan's fate was simple and blunt. The victors said, in effect, that Japan had got itself into a mess and it was up to the Japanese to repair the damage at home and abroad. We noted earlier that, while such an approach lingered on in some quarters until the 1950s, it was quickly superseded in American official thinking. Japan was too important a prize to be put at risk. Revenge was forgotten. Reconstruction took its place. The Japanese government could only benefit from this rapid change of heart. It knew it was assured of American subsidies and food shipments and could (and did) pass the buck when economic mismanagement emerged. There was indeed much for the United States to criticize. Low productivity, high inflation, careless bookkeeping and a vast black economy were all part of the picture. Yet a gradual and patchy improvement did appear after 1948. This was an achievement in itself, given that the dislocations of the first post-surrender months had left GNP for 1946 as low as the 1917–18 level.

Management of the Japanese economy during the occupation retained many familiar features of the 1930s and the Pacific war era. Government direction was widespread throughout whole sectors. There was continuity of institution and policy – made all the easier by the infrequency of purges within the civil service. The national bureaucracy ended the occupation as firmly entrenched as ever. This was unfortunate but predictable when, for instance, ministers in the inexperienced Katayama cabinet had to have their hands held by their vice-ministers. Guidance to politicians and industrialists both before and after the occupation followed in the same groove. The objectives of the first three years were only partially achieved. Getting people back to work and encouraging manufacturers to invest stoked up inflation and produced vigorous complaints and direct action from newly formed trades unions. SCAP by 1947 then began to reconsider its attitude towards labour and in 1948 the civil service unions were stripped of their right to strike. Efforts were also made to persuade the Japanese government to come to grips with its budgetary problems. If labour was disappointed with MacArthur's actions, the Japanese economic bureaucracy had to swallow its share of bitter medicine in 1949 when the so-called 'Dodge Line' was imposed on the economy. That it was required at all is an indictment of Japan's civil servants who had made the appropriate noises on price stabilization programmes but gave official preference to increasing national output. Under the Dodge programme – named after the Detroit banker who led the American survey mission at the personal request of President Truman – Japan was obliged to follow an austerity package that its bureaucrats had lacked the courage to recommend to their masters. Dodge's attacks on tax evasion, budget deficits and an inflation rate which was wiping out industry's debts suggest that much was amiss with the Japanese economy and its overseers.

Economic recovery was assisted by United States aid. The American journalist John Gunther was told in 1950 that 'the contemporary Japanese prayer is that God grant that the United States should cease to be their overlord but continue to be their underwriter'. Millions of dollars of aid helped keep the economy afloat, since Japan's foreign currency earnings could hardly begin to pay for its essential imports of food and raw materials. When a unified foreign currency system eventually began in 1949, with a fixed exchange rate of ¥360 to the dollar, many observers held that the yen had been deliberately undervalued to assist Japanese exporters in their struggle to recapture Asian and African markets. The British, for one, were not amused.

The outbreak of the Korean war in June 1950 was a godsend to the economy. The United States suddenly required the services of Japanese manufacturers and construction companies. Material for the Eighth Army and Fifth Air Force brought in valuable dollars. American 'special procurements' paid for half of Japan's imports in 1952. The Korean war-boom permitted the economy to take off at the same time as the country regained its independence. Fortune certainly had favoured Japan; the Japanese made the most of their good luck. Expansion continued. From 1953 onwards the managers of the Japanese economy were in unfamiliar territory, since the old benchmarks had been passed. The rest of the 1950s produced an unprecedented boom accompanied by a short recession in 1957–8. The high growth era was underway.

It is tempting to describe much of Japan's economic history from the mid 1950s to the mid 1980s as pre-ordained. Yet success was far from inevitable. The same popular ingredients were, of course, present throughout but there were always alternative bureaucratic options and paths not taken. Prime Minister Yoshida, for example, during the last months of his lengthy period in office threw out MITI's proposed schemes to develop Japan's heavy industrial potential. The schemes were, however, approved after his resignation. The twin objectives were to strengthen Japan's industrial structure, which in turn would generate exports and hopefully pay for the required raw materials, and to develop a larger domestic market for consumer goods. A nation that had subsisted on a military footing for a generation as either occupier or occupied was at last to gain some relaxation, but the relatively low priority given to personal consumption is testimony alike to government psychology and public patience.

Expansion both at home and overseas led to an annual economic growth rate in the late 1950s of approximately 8%. This in its turn gave the Ikeda cabinet sufficient confidence to approve a much-heralded 'National Income Doubling Plan' in December 1960. Here was evidence, if the remaining doubters were prepared to take off their blinkers, that Japan meant business. The 1950s had provided the industrial foundations in steel, chemicals and shipbuilding on which later prosperity could be built. The Western image of Japan as the alarm clock and bicycle exporter was hopelessly out of date by 1960. Yet it persisted. De Gaulle is reputed to have said he was going to have a little chat with a Japanese transistor salesman. He meant rather an interview with the premier of the nation which in 1962 had a larger gross national product than France.

The 1960s showed growth acceleration that left even the record of the late 1950s in the shade. For manufacturing industries these were to be the sweet years. By the end of the decade Japan ranked number one in shipbuilding, radio and television production and was third in crude steel, pulp, cement, fertilizer and passenger-car output. Productivity increases permitted industrialists to plough back their profits in the shape of more modern equipment, which in its turn boosted production. During the early 1960s foreign journalists began to attach the epithet 'miracle' to stories filed from Tokyo. Gradually, some popular perceptions began to change. It would prove to be an all too brief period of Western applause before trade hostilities commenced.

If the media overseas were starting to take note of Japan, changes were also underway in Japan's external trade relations. Pressure began to mount from other industrialized nations to persuade Japan to liberalize its currency and open up its domestic markets. Behaviour that had been tolerated when the Japanese economy was under reconstruction could find relatively few defenders by 1960, and fewer still later when the pace of change continued to be slow. The Japanese government's approach to international criticism was to wait until the pressure became intense and then respond with the bare minimum likely to get the West temporarily to relent. Japan's propensity to import finished goods was low, and even in the 1980s has remained disappointing. Japanese tariffs until the 1970s were calculated to dissuade Japanese trading companies from importing foreign-manufactured goods that were currently available within Japan.

The government simultaneously built up nascent manufacturing industries behind high tariff walls. Many would contend that the Japanese car industry might never have attained its present global position without highly protectionist barriers in the 1950s and 1960s. It was often the case that the size of the rapidly expanding home market was sufficient to launch and then develop a product before attempts were made to crack overseas markets. Internationalization was seen by Japan's economic bureaucracy as something to be avoided until there were sufficiently competitive domestic industries able to fend off any likely foreign challenge. The evidence from a series of economic plans in the 1960s and early 1970s would suggest that neither the government nor the public at large had any quarrel with such nationalistic trade strategies. The 'promotion of international co-operation' was invariably the item consigned to the end of government economic and social planning reports.

Dynamic growth continued until 1973. Japan's foreign trade expanded at a formidable rate, unmatched by any other advanced nation. The arguments that some had applied to the fast growth of the 1950s were quickly shown to be out of date. The dislocations of war and the determination to recover did not lead to any reduction in economic performance once Japan had put itself back on its feet. Quite the reverse. Exports, which had totalled $4,100 million in 1960, reached $19,300 million in 1970 and by 1973 had increased to $36,900 million. For the period 1960–70 Japan's annual growth rate exceeded 10% throughout the decade, aside from two short recessions in 1962 and 1965.

Even at the bottom of the business cycle the economy continued to experience a creditable growth rate. Manufacturing industries, aided by remarkably high re-investment in new machinery, boomed. Where it had been unusual to find household appliances such as electric washing machines, refrigerators, cleaners and sewing machines in Japanese homes in the 1950s, it was rare indeed a generation later to enter houses without all of these consumer items. Demand for colour television and air conditioning also mushroomed with exporters again concentrating first on the domestic market and then preparing aggressive export drives at highly competitive prices. On the basis of such successes, economists began to pose very different questions from those of a decade earlier. Instead of asking when the Japanese boom would peter out, the issue became rather to estimate when Japan might conceivably surpass the United States. The talk was of the Japanese century and double digit economic growth through the 1980s and beyond.

It did not work out quite that way. International events beyond Japan's control quickly and unceremoniously aborted some of these wilder predictions. Simultaneously, economists began to refer to that suspiciously vague phrase, beloved of politicians, 'the quality of life'. It was (with hindsight) as if the ending of the supergrowth years had been replaced overnight by a new and seemingly more worthy human goal. Reference to 'domestic socio-economic structural change' and a Japanese 'welfare society' coincided with what the Japanese press termed the 'Oil Shock'. The economy, which was already in difficulties through Prime Minister Tanaka's ambitious yet inflationary political schemes, an undervalued yen and excess liquidity, temporarily slumped. It would soon recover, but the impact on Japan of the Arab oil embargo of the autumn of 1973 was profound. The public was being told that growth was not necessarily beneficial at the same time as it had to swallow an inflation rate in 1973 of 29%. No wonder it was to look back nostalgically on the growth years, when the rest of the world was not breathing down Japan's neck and the social consequences of fast industrialization were not so readily appreciated. As Edwin Reischauer, the former American ambassador to Tokyo, aptly noted of the Oil Shock's impact on the Japanese: 'For them the world would never seem the same again'.

Yet new slogans rapidly replaced the old. The situational ethic which had assisted in digesting the traumas of defeat and occupation played its part in the public's accommodation of uncomfortable realities in the 1970s. If the quadrupling of oil prices achieved nothing else, it did provide a salutary reminder that Japan was no longer an island relatively free from foreign contacts. The aim now was to 'internationalize' Japan. The concept was decidedly leaky but it surely pointed out what ought to have been obvious earlier, yet had been continually played down by the government and the civil service. Japan, after its first Oil Shock, needed to win friends and influence states that it had previously regarded as little more than export markets or sources of cheap fuels and primary products. It had to begin to implement many of the existing paper commitments to liberalize its complicated import system and let other nations stake a claim to a share of the enticing but difficult Japanese domestic market. It had, in effect, to change its behaviour.

It is tempting, but more than a little unfair, to deride this switch as sheer opportunism masquerading as talk of new international orders and global interdependence. The Japanese government's policies were probably no better or no worse than those of other industrialized nations facing the threat of energy and resource shortages. Its responsibilities lay primarily with its citizens and their livelihood. To safeguard Japan's economic future it was obliged to reconsider its Middle Eastern diplomacy, talk publicly and work privately for trade and capital liberalization and convince Japan's business and bureaucratic élites that trade surpluses and non-tariff barriers might cause more problems than they attempted to solve. The period from the mid 1970s to the end of the decade might, therefore, be termed the era of re-assessment. It was the occasion when Japan was obliged to review its postwar history and re-evaluate its standing.

Japan came out of the 1970s in far better shape than either its economic bureaucrats or foreign friends could have dared to imagine in 1974. Two Oil Shocks had been overcome, most of its industries – the exceptions were sometimes important – had been opened up to overseas competition, and Japan had begun to make its first hesitant moves to export its capital to the West as well as to developing nations. Such measures were intended to emphasize Japan's new appreciation of its responsibilities to the contemporary international economy. The rest of the world took a more cautious view. It was still unprepared to share the optimism of the Japanese economist who could write in 1976 that 'the period of a disproportionate impact of Japan's economic growth on the world must now be assumed to belong to the past'.

Later events have left a host of international economic issues still unresolved. Japan, in the meantime, has emerged once more as a nation with an impressive economic record. Growth has been considerable by the standards of its main trading rivals. While western Europe and North America were still submerged in their worst depression since the 1930s, Japan had experienced an export-led recovery by 1983. The air, once again, was thick with charges of Japanese malpractices and immediate denials from MITI and MOF. It was apparent, however, that many of the less well-informed attacks on Japanese economic practices were no longer being taken as seriously as they might have been in the past. The Japanese economy was a different animal from that of a decade earlier. Tokyo had a stronger case by the 1980s and was becoming more skilful at presenting its arguments.

The contrast between the affluent and increasingly assertive Japan of the mid 1980s and the austerity of the occupation years is self-evident. Yet younger Japanese who have known nothing but prosperity find accounts of postwar deprivation of little interest. The Pacific war is recalled for the public every year with massive media attention on the anniversary of the atomic bombing of Hiroshima, but no group in Japanese society has any vested interest in recalling the indignities and hardship of the first decade after surrender. There is a large gap in the collective memory between the last days of the war and the beginnings of a more comfortable existence, which might be dated popularly somewhere between the marriage of the Crown Prince in 1959 and the Tokyo Olympics in 1964.

Certainly by the early 1960s Japan was on the way up again. Its recovery was over and the economy was now enjoying the benefits of what one Japanese economist and former foreign minister has termed 'the virtuous circle of accelerated growth'. Japan had made it. Or so it appeared; but had it? Our subjective verdict will depend on the answers to two questions. The first is to ask whether the costs of economic development outweigh the benefits to Japan. The second will place the Japanese record within an international context and use European and North American standards, since Japan itself has long wished to be judged by such comparisons.

National reconstruction was the undoubted goal of Japan after the exhilarating initial successes and the later retreats of the Pacific war had ended in total capitulation. There were, of course, major differences between Japanese political groups as to how the economy ought to be organized and its fruits distributed, but few citizens needed to be reminded of Japan's predicament. Gaining sufficient funds to purchase food and fuel was most people's primary interest. Trades unions had much to complain about, but their leaders, in an admittedly difficult period, were generally a disappointment. The conservatives' election victory in 1949 was an indictment of the Katayama minority government and its labour supporters. Yoshida's new mandate, however, did not ensure any better economic future for Japan, since, even with his acceptance of the stabilization programme insisted upon by the United States, the outlook appeared grim. American diplomats were informed that Japan would have to put up with 'a deficit economy in precarious straits for years to come'. The Japanese smallholder, now working in his own minute fields, and the urban clerk in his rented wooden house, equipped with an earth closet and cold tap, knew this only too well.

Economic difficulties remained throughout the 1950s. The stress on capital investment was remarkable ('investment invites more investment' was the slogan of the 1961 white paper from the Economic Planning Agency), though the generation to gain most from such endeavours were the children of parents who put in the long hours in factories and offices after the war. There was a lengthy and quite deliberate time-lag before the Japanese government and its officials gave serious thought to much beyond higher wages. As the young novelist Ishiguro Kazuo was to write later of the occupants of a new jerry-built apartment block in Nagasaki during the 1950s, 'we were all of us waiting for the day we could move to something better'.

Critics of Yoshida complained that 'everything was economy, everything was efficiency'. Yet the election returns for the next two decades make it apparent that this had broad popular appeal. The left might warn of remilitarization and subordinate independence under the American anti-Communist banner in Asia, but the conservatives moved slowly over defence and took pains to minimize budgetary allocations to the Self-Defence Forces. The Income-Doubling Plan of 1960 was highly popular and 'wildly overfulfilled'. It was now the turn of the 'three Cs' (car, cooler and colour TV) to replace the 'three Sacred Treasures' (washing machine, refrigerator and black and white TV). Unemployment was minimal, wages and savings ratios were up and the Japanese Housing Corporation's first apartment complexes were being rented to those fortunate enough to qualify. The opening of the Shinkansen bullet train service between Tokyo and Osaka in October 1964, to coincide with the Tokyo Olympics, was further confirmation of Japanese engineering prowess and the occasion for not a little self-congratulation. The fastest train network in the world and an economy shortly to overtake West Germany's suggested, as one Japanese novelist wrote of the opening ceremonies of the Olympics, that 'Japan had finally regained its national competency'.

The last major Japanese prestige event before a greater awareness of the strains of industrialization emerged was EXPO '70. It is a convenient symbol of where Japan stood on the eve of global currency and fuel crises. The crowds at the international exhibition site near Osaka were vast, patient and uncritical. It was a mass celebration of an urban future that was swamped by too many people in too small a space. The carnival for Japan was soon to be temporarily over. The 1970s were to be harder years.

It was time to take stock. The Japanese people had worked their passage back from poverty to a formidable ranking in the international economic pecking order. Yet, obviously, the size of the economy was no more than one yardstick by which to determine the state of the nation. Critics could suggest that incidences of poverty, income distribution statistics, per capita wealth, housing conditions, the extent of social mobility and size of welfare payments presented a less rosy picture. There was a degree of truth in all these complaints. The government had ignored social infrastructure in order that industry should receive first priority. Metropolitan housing and recreational facilities were inadequate. Pensions were small. Still, popular perceptions were not greatly changed by press and opposition to what has been termed 'social deprivation'. Public opinion polls have shown that the bulk of the Japanese people have since the late 1960s seen themselves as middle-class. Overseas commentators were often struck more by the lack of urban initiative to demand improvement in the face of environmental and housing deficiencies than the vigour of protest movements. Acquiescence was the usual response. Improved salaries left most Japanese unmoved by the thought of collective action. The economy might have its shortcomings but few wished personally to confront these consequences.

The left's theoreticians had reason enough to castigate the Japanese government for playing down the social costs of economic growth until the 1970s. There were serious gaps in some areas of what, rather late in the day, aspires to be a 'welfare society'. Much has since altered for the better. Yet these improvements have been not infrequently overlooked in the West. European opinion maintains, to quote the *Economist*'s special survey on Japan in July 1983, that 'Japan's infrastructure is little better than a developing country's'. The reality is less damning and likely to continue to improve as Japan appears capable of an annual growth rate for the remainder of the 1980s of 3–4%.

'Quality of life' is a suggestive phrase but one perhaps capable of only approximate definition. Its advocates at times offer it as a synonym for the welfare state or as a stick with which to beat free-market economists. For our purposes it will be employed to reflect changing social and political values, which lay less stress on production *per se* as Japan hesitantly ponders the consequences of its rapid industrialization. Two cautions must immediately be noted. Economic growth is still the popular aspiration and the doubts implied in 'quality of life' criticisms are not widespread. Japan's own breed of capitalism is not under siege. (Historians, as 'Mr Dooley' said of the American Supreme Court, are obliged to follow the election returns.) Secondly, if social welfare is inadequate in some areas, there are other indicators that show Japan in a favourable light by even the most rigorous international comparison.

Health and education are two important social welfare provisions in which Japan has been up with the frontrunners, if not ahead of the pack. Life expectancy for the Japanese is among the highest in the world. For females only Iceland may slightly exceed the average Japanese life expectancy at birth of 79.1 years. For males Japan appears to have the record for longevity (73.8 years). We shall look later at the demographic changes in store for Japan over the next two generations and the effects this will probably have on Japanese society in general. For the moment we can assume that improved postwar medical care and dietary changes have contributed to a nation that is now living 30 years longer than its citizens born at the end of the Taisho period (1926). Japan's provision of hospital beds per thousand people was the highest in the world in 1970, though its number of doctors was lower than its hospital record might suggest. Still, hospital care is good, particularly at the infant level. (Older doctors keep their medical records in German.)

Improvements in education can be welcomed, though here again qualification will be necessary later. The change in length of education received by differing age groups within Japanese society is instructive and a source of considerable pride. In 1980, 37.9% of the relevant age group were attending some form of tertiary education. The mass diploma society had arrived. While further diffusion of higher education will probably grow more slowly in the future, the percentage of youths continuing on to senior high school (at the age of 15) has already reached 94.3%. This level is far in excess of the situation that exists in some English-speaking countries.

Japan has also a first-class inter-city train network. After the Tokyo–Osaka line was completed, the Shinkansen spread south to Kyushu and later in 1983 north and westwards. The more rural regions are clearly benefiting from their improved communications with the Tokyo–Nagoya–Osaka industrial centres. The service is fast, punctual and safe. In addition, national highways (currently totalling 3,000 km) have been constructed, often to run in the same narrow coastal belt parallel to the Shinkansen. Passengers and goods can be transported at high speed from one urban centre to the next, but neither commuters nor freight-liners can avoid the inner urban congestion. The roads into the city centres on weekdays (Monday to Saturday still for many Japanese) are rarely less than crowded, while the situation on commuter trains from the suburbs to business districts is indeed an endurance test. Commuting depends equally on the efficiency of the train system and the tolerance of its passengers. The service is fast, punctual and unpleasant.

Writing in 1958, Kenneth Galbraith began the first page of his work *The Affluent Society* by defining the nations of wealth as those 'in the comparatively small corner of the world populated by Europeans'. Neither there nor anywhere else in his book did Japan receive any recognition. It was to be slightly different 15 years later when he published *Economics and the Public Purpose* and surely impossible by the 1980s to ignore Japan in any extended discussion of contemporary economic development. European and North American interest in Japan's present economic position – a combination of admiration and secret longing that Japan might slip up on its own banana skin – has greatly increased since the days of *The Affluent Society* and will, we may safely assume, continue to do so.

Galbraith (who was involved in the United States Strategic Bombing Survey of Germany and Japan at the end of the war) might, however, be a convenient source of some strictures against the Japan of the first three postwar decades. The god of production had few rivals and certainly no equal. Higher growth was a national obsession and is still an essential goal. The attention given to a continuing spate of governmental and private economic forecasts by the press confirms this. There was, and there undoubtedly remains, considerable wariness against public expenditure. Much of Galbraith's anger at the United States of the Edsel Era (Ford's ill-fated model was launched in the same week as the Soviet Union put the Sputnik into space) could be applied to the Japan of the high growth era. Civic amenities were played down, roads were built without much thought as to whether a slow-moving stream of cars into Tokyo did anything but pollute an already noxious atmosphere and manufacturers refused to imagine there might be a finite number to the electrical goods that the Japanese household could be persuaded to purchase. The market has clearly not achieved all that the Keidanren would have us believe. The result is the lop-sided Japan of today.

Since then, however, the worst pollution problems have been overcome. Japan's present fuel exhaust regulations are stricter than Britain's. Photo-chemical smog has disappeared. (The idea that Tokyo's traffic policemen are obliged to wear oxygen masks to survive is another firmly entrenched foreign myth.) At last the sewage system is also being improved and the habit of connecting effluent and storm drains is on the way out. It is not going to make headlines or win a single vote, but one of Japan's more laudable goals is to attain European levels of sewage disposal by the year 2000. Equally sensible are plans gradually to enlarge the park and recreational levels in Japan's metropolitan wastelands. 'Green Associations' are in their infancy (modelled on Britain's National Trust), yet they too demonstrate a belated attempt to prevent the total denuding of what remains of the natural environment on the outskirts of the urban complexes. Public attitudes may be slowly changing and politicians at both the national and local level appear to be readier to listen. It can at least be said that the rhetoric has altered. Prime Minister Nakasone refers to 'environmental beautification'.

Substantial improvement has since been underway in a variety of fields, which may collectively be described as contributing to the betterment of Japan's 'quality of life'. Health, education, the urban environment and housing are widely accepted criteria that help determine what article 25 of the Constitution calls 'the promotion and extension of social welfare and security'. The advances made possible here by economic growth have been very considerable. Gaps, it is certainly true, remain, but it seems reasonable to assume that a gradual improvement in such areas as metropolitan housing may be possible. Appearances, too, can be slightly misleading. Visitors arriving armed with phrases such as 'rabbit hutches' may be in danger of prejudging Japan's largest city.

Tokyo is admittedly an urban planner's nightmare. The capital's unprepossessing appearance is legendary. Yet this façade disguises a different reality of a metropolis with immense strengths and resilience. Grandparents who can recall the Kanto earthquake of 1923, the fire-bombings that devastated whole sections of the city in 1945 and the early postwar austerity have reason to boast. Ignore the skyscrapers of the central business districts – awash with blue suits during the day – and downtown Tokyo is a patchwork of bath houses, *pachinko* parlours, stand bars and tenements, in competition with factories, timberyards, offices and school playgrounds for the precious space. Motorways (constructed for the 1964 Tokyo Olympics) weave over-head to add to the noise and neon. It is rarely pretty, but Tokyo is undeniably alive in contrast to some European and American inner cities.

Only slightly less higgledy-piggledy lie the suburbs. Here bicycle lots threaten to engulf the train stations and two-storey tiled houses, fish shops, company dormitories and yet more bars offer respite of a kind to commuters who face uncomfortable journeys of one and a half hours to and from work. Further out still, in what remains of Tokyo's rural hinterland, the silence and darkness in the evenings is near total. Every spring, as yet safely beyond the steadily encroaching sprawl, farming families fly giant carp bunting in anticipation of the Boys' Day festival and perhaps also to celebrate their escape.

Similar urban transformation has occurred throughout Japan. Indeed, practically the entire narrow eastern coastal strip from Tokyo down to Hiroshima is in danger of becoming one contiguous built-up zone. It is not a pleasant prospect. The constant employment of stan-dardized woodboard and plastics has left many areas, without the urban traditions of a Tokyo or Osaka, a wasteland. Seemingly uncon-trolled development – without the slightest aesthetic pretence – has achieved little more than a series of miniature Ginzas for the enjoyment of newly urbanized citizens living in quickly made and easily demolished flats and houses. Japan as its tourist information offices might wish it to be has largely disappeared.

4

Japan's external relations

Japan is a potential great power. In terms of economic stature its place in the sun is clear. Its relatively low military posture, its limited cultural diplomacy and the general figure it cuts on the international scene cannot at present, however, be regarded as behaviour comparable to today's superpowers. Some of this may be changing as the Japanese government reconsiders its nation's role in world affairs and encourages discussion over Japan's future military, diplomatic and economic options. While Japan is not likely to become a nuclear power, it is seemingly set on creating a larger and more articulate external policy. We shall look here at how Japan's postwar foreign relations have evolved and assess the possible direction of future Japanese diplomacy.

We will have to be careful not to overstate our case. Japanese foreign policy initiatives since the war have been more noted for their absence than novelty or frequency. If major change is likely to emerge, it follows, therefore, that a number of deeply embedded attitudes (termed by some as 'taboos') will have to be scrapped. To take but one example of hesitancy from the autumn of 1983. Following the shooting down of the Korean airliner inside Soviet airspace, the Japanese government was loud in condemnation of the Soviet Union but reluctant to go beyond verbal attacks. The foreign ministry blew hot and cold. It was eager to criticize Moscow since Japanese citizens had died in the incident, yet the cabinet was not prepared at first to call for sanctions or take any leading role in discussions among Western governments. The Japanese spokesman fell back on a phrase which all too often has characterized Japan's response to international affairs since 1952; he said that any retaliatory measures that might 'eventually' be imposed by Japan would be dependent on 'closely observing domestic and international opinions'. The action initially decided upon – to prohibit Japanese civil servants from flying with Aeroflot – was no more than the mildest of slaps on the wrist. All this was predictable and in keeping with past Japanese caution.

While the cabinet determined its position over the Korean airliner affair, Prime Minister Nakasone gave a policy address to the 100th session of the Diet. In this he stated that 'international hopes and expectations of Japan are growing rapidly. It will become increasingly difficult for Japan to attain a stable place in the international community if we ignore such trends'. Yet any translation of such overseas opinion into action may not be easy. It will be necessary in this section to distinguish between the objectives of the Japanese government, popular perceptions and the hopes of Japan's allies, since all three may have different views on any future external role for Japan.

First the domestic context. We need to remind ourselves that the Japanese people have not forgotten the Pacific war. The lesson that public opinion has continued to draw from the militarist era is still clear. Some would suggest that this message must inevitably fade in the next two decades but that may be to ignore the ability of families and political associations to recall the war years for younger Japanese. The crescendo of publicity every year culminating on the anniversaries of the atomic bombing of Hiroshima and Nagasaki ought not to be ignored when analysts call for a more rational defence policy and speak of the need to define a comprehensive national security programme for Japan. At the very least it might suggest that some political views should be tampered with only after considerable effort has been made at public persuasion. The contemporary Japanese soldier is not a figure held in high esteem, thanks to the behaviour of his grandfather's generation.

Hatred of war, often without regard to Japan's geographic or strategic position in east Asia, is a strong restraint on any Japanese governmental hopes of increasing its military spending or enlarging its off-shore defence responsibilities. The Self-Defence Forces (SDF) are more usually seen by the public as an auxiliary unit to be called upon to assist in coping with Japan's frequent natural disasters than a fighting force capable of defending Japan's borders. It is more the image of the soldier as back-up fire-fighter or flood-controller than peace-keeper. The difficulties that the SDF has over recruitment, the reluctance of farmers to co-operate over training and munition storage plans and the wall of hostility it must attempt to surmount in explaining its mission to a sceptical public remain.

The strongest evidence against any substantial military build-up is the need for successive Japanese prime ministers (whatever their personal views on defence) to pledge their commitment to restrain military expenditure to 1% of GNP. This is, indeed, a sacred cow. It has grown in importance over the last decade and is regarded by the public as an article of faith. It certainly makes the preparation of a defence budget more difficult and has led to vociferous complaints from the United States. The 1% figure, when combined with Japan's constitutional restraints on expanding beyond self-defence and the government's continuing opposition to Japan's manufacture and possession of nuclear weapons, would appear to limit severely any substantial growth of Japanese militarism now or in the future. There are certainly strains on Japanese pacifism but relatively few of them can be said to originate from the public at large. The Japanese people may be oblivious to many present realities of international relations in northeast Asia but they do know only too well what happened last time Japan sought to dominate the Pacific. The seemingly endless foreign concern over if and when Japan might decide to go nuclear is understandable but somewhat unrealistic in the light of the state of Japanese domestic sentiment. It would take major changes in the power rivalries of the region and considerable enlargement of the nuclear club before the issue left the realm of conjecture. Today it is not on the cards.

Japanese public sentiment is one of a number of factors to be considered in any discussion of Japan's foreign policy. The relatively unchanging attitude of the Japanese people – cutting across political allegiance – has proved both a source of consistency and a problem for successive LDP administrations. Having been at peace for the past four decades it would be very difficult to convince the public of the advantages of substantially increased military spending or alterations to the 'peace' constitution of 1947. Japan said goodbye to its expansionist past in August 1945 and is not to be easily tempted to travel down the same road again. The metamorphosis has been too successful for significant political groups to garner support for alternative policies. Japan has no military–industrial complex and the climate of opinion today would be wary of spokesmen who claimed the need for such a development.

All this makes the preparation of a coherent foreign policy fraught with difficulty. Public opinion appreciates only too well the blessings of peace and feels that by remaining a non-nuclear, lightly armed nation it may continue to avoid the the conflicts which have been a prominent feature of the postwar Asian political scene. The government's responsibilities have, of course, to take note of far wider and more complex realities. It cannot afford merely to follow the head-in-the-sand approach of public opinion. Yet any strong challenge to the present orthodoxy of limiting Japanese rearmament and stressing the economic dimension of foreign policy is unlikely to achieve the desired results. The media and most opposition parties would create sufficient furor to oblige the government to retract its statements. In Japan change is more often incremental. Gradualism can win where confrontation will fail.

What then are the outlines of contemporary Japanese external relations and how might they be altered in the medium term? The Japanese Diplomatic Bluebook for 1981 stated that 'the mission of Japan's foreign policy is to protect liberty and democracy, the basic values on which our nation stands, and to ensure a safe and affluent livelihood for our people'. (Japan has come a long way since the dark days of 1945 when any such sentiments from the Foreign Ministry could hardly have been envisaged.) To achieve such goals the Japanese government has continued to stress its partnership with the United States, which was first formalized by the 1952 security pact, and to strengthen its economic ties with the Western industrial powers, the Middle East and what was formerly termed the Third World. It has also constantly to keep in mind its geopolitical position in northeast Asia *vis-à-vis* the Soviet Union, China and a divided Korea.

Japan's relationship with the United States is unquestionably 'the cornerstone of its diplomacy'. This apparently unlikely alliance has endured since the occupation and it would be unwise to imagine that the undoubted relative decline in American power in the Pacific region might lead to its future demise. What is more probable is that there will be more strident calls from the United States for a greater Japanese defence effort in the light of improved Soviet military capabilities. Whether Tokyo will respond significantly to approaches from the United States for a continuous build-up in its SDF is problematic, given the state of Japanese public opinion. Any Japanese cabinet would be tempted under such domestic circumstances to offer alternative proposals to the United States, which might stress Japan's reservations over re-equipping its forces and suggest instead additional economic assistance to supposedly deserving nations.

The US–Japan relationship, despite the past strains over the nature of the security treaty, the problems associated with the reversion of Okinawa and difficulties inherent in the mere American presence through bases on Japanese soil, has survived to embarrass its many opponents. The Japanese left, however, will continue to remain unimpressed and critics within the United States will persist in denouncing the arrangement as a 'free ride' for Japan whereby Tokyo gains protection on the cheap. European eyebrows are likely to be raised too by the constant reference of Ambassador Mike Mansfield to the 'US–Japan partnership' as 'the most important bilateral relationship in the world, bar none'. (It would be intriguing to learn of Mrs Thatcher's response to such harping on Pacific bonds.) Doubts abound over such sentiments when Japanese public opinion surveys demonstrate great scepticism over being able to rely on American protection should Japan be threatened militarily and American attitudes towards Japan may be hardening in the light of Japanese balance of payments surpluses and hesitancy over increased defence expenditure.

Why then has the arrangement, which was undeniably a forced marriage in the 1950s, persisted? Obviously because both governments have found sufficient advantages in the relationship to overlook the faults inherent in any alliance. The scheme has evolved considerably from the days when Japan was poor and uncertain of its future in a hostile environment of Communist neighbours and sceptical ex-enemy nations. Today more is certainly expected from Japan. Prime Minister Nakasone has earned American goodwill through his public statements on aligning Japan with the West, but any action will be harder to achieve. The United States may be finding the defence of its allies in Asia a larger task than it can fulfil without Japanese assistance, yet the SDF is hardly capable at present of doing much beyond temporarily delaying any Soviet aggression and must put its faith in the United States coming to the rescue. The present 'nuclear fiction' that the Japanese government is unaware of the introduction of American nuclear weapons into Japanese waters leaves the entire debate of what response Tokyo might expect from the United States a non-starter. Much of the discussion in Japanese circles on defence and foreign policy has a similar air of unreality about it. Figures on the left talk of waving white flags, while the government dislikes doing anything that might give the impression of any weakening of the all-important issue of civilian control. (Sensitivity on this score has ensured that no military figures have a seat on the National Defence Council that advises the prime minister on defence issues.)

The two parallel responses of American irritation and understanding of the domestic background to Japanese foreign policy are likely to persist. Japan has put its trust in the United States since 1952 and, while it may have other options for the future depending on the international situation in east Asia and beyond, it is not about to make any dramatic changes in its basic orientation. It must expect, however, shortly to provide more tangible action on means to cement the alliance. The days when one rationale behind American ties with Japan was to ensure that Japan itself did not once again threaten the Pacific are long gone. The United States, for example, is eager for the Japanese Maritime Self-Defence Force to move beyond its coastguard mentality to co-operate in patrolling the sea lanes between the South China Sea and Japanese territorial waters. The deployment of more modern missiles is also being strongly pressed by the Pentagon, if the Japanese government is serious about defending its territory. Yet at a time of government budgetary retrenchment, it will take considerable political courage to persist in any prolonged expansion of SDF expenditure.

The drawbacks to Japan's current defence thinking are echoed in its foreign policy. Much of Japan's postwar external relations have been essentially passive, leading to cynical queries as to whether the Japanese government could be said to have anything worthy of the name of a foreign policy. Its claim to be concerned over East–West and North–South problems has not always been met with quite the applause the foreign ministry might have hoped for, while its statements on its readiness to co-operate with the other advanced industrial nations of the West would win an unsympathetic hearing in Detroit or Duisburg. Yet, if Japan has remained largely an adaptive power that shifts as international circumstances alter, it has achieved a rare degree of success for a state that has remained a minor military nation in an international system based on force. Having achieved so much in such a short time, it would be strange indeed if the Japanese public would immediately wish to alter its diplomatic stance merely to satisfy overseas powers. Those who encourage Japan to play a larger role in regional affairs and beyond have first to convince sizeable portions of its electorate. The public, unfortunately for some, has been long accustomed to invoking the defensive nature of its undermanned and underequipped military forces and thinks of Japan exclusively as an economic power standing equidistant between power blocs while seeking to pose a threat to no one.

Politicians are rarely brave or foolhardy enough to jettison popular policies for the sake of acquiring a larger role, in this instance, in international affairs, unless it can be demonstrated that the exercise is likely to be in its people's own interests. This will not be easy and the LDP may be tempted to risk the wrath of the United States and western Europe rather than comply in earnest. Japan has been slow or unwilling to perceive what some see as an expanding Soviet 'threat' to east Asia. It has likewise been largely unsympathetic to complaints made by co-members of the West's economic summit that it shares a substantial responsibility to assist in rekindling world economic growth. The Japanese public would undoubtedly prefer its government's foreign policy to concentrate on solving economic issues and avoid entangling alliances that might have unforeseen complications. It wants, in effect, the world to ignore Japan's existence as anything more than a trading nation. The rest of the world has no intention of doing anything of the kind. Japan, whether it likes or not, is an important factor in the global balance of power. The United States has been unwilling since 1945 to release its hold on Japan, though it would never in the 1980s use such intemperate language, since Japan is a prize that it will continue to deny to the Soviet Union. The industrial strength and military potential of Japan is such as to ensure that Japanese activities will be most carefully watched and analysed in east Asian capitals and beyond.

The economic dimension of Japanese external relations has clearly been the basis of Japan's postwar dealings with the rest of the world. It is unlikely that this rather single-minded approach can be quickly corrected and the rhetoric about Japan assuming a more extensive international role remains suspect. The detailed public opinion survey conducted by the prime minister's office in June 1983 confirmed that, while 39% of those questioned thought that the United States should be the nation to which Japan ought to have the friendliest of relations, 14% wished for amicable ties with all states and an additional 20% either did not know or considered no particular state ought to be singled out in such a manner. For the moment then it might be advisable to treat some suggestions that Japanese perceptions of the world have changed with caution.

It will take time for popular opinion to be convinced that the United States' security guarantees to Japan have to be earned, rather than assumed to apply automatically in all circumstances regardless of Japan's own military endeavours. The idea of Japan as a trading nation that has departed from the messy world of Realpolitik still applies. The opinions of the left-wing study group that thought in 1950 that 'Japan must firmly maintain the policy of strictly avoiding interference or involvement in any international dispute' continues to be widely endorsed. Innocence has not yet been lost. Moralism, drawn from one strand of the American foreign policy tradition, is far from extinguished. The bloodbaths of postwar Asia tend to be ignored and the dangers of resource scarcity and envy in developing states forgotten. Japan's prewar insistence on its own 'have not' status does not engender any significant concern for the fate of the newly independent nations of today.

Japan's recognition of its own economic vulnerability is certain to remain an important basis for its foreign policy. Dangerous exposure to international pressure if, for example, another and more serious oil embargo were to be applied by OPEC members could cripple entire sectors of its economy. It is widely claimed that Japan's lack of self-sufficiency in some foodstuffs (rice is an important exception) and its energy and raw materials deficiencies have to be constantly borne in mind when Japan approaches the rest of the world. The supposed fragility of the Japanese economy is never far from the surface in the minds of Japanese diplomats. Is Japan then a 'fragile glass tower'? Are its problems in a unique category that merits special consideration from other states?

Statistical evidence would appear to support parts of what is an *idée fixe* of the Japanese public. The absence of crude petroleum and iron ore, coupled with limited indigenous supplies of coal and natural gas, ensures that Japanese industry must import to survive. Nearly three-quarters of Japan's imports are accounted for by mineral fuels (41% in 1979), other raw materials (20%) and foodstuffs (12%). The strength of the Japanese economy, however, makes it possible for Japan to gain advantageous long-term contracts with a variety of overseas sources that often reduce the risks that colour much popular thinking. Japan, of course, faces the constant danger of oil disruption from its Middle Eastern suppliers through political turmoil in the region, blockade or conflict along the sea lanes, but it is far from the only nation with such nightmares. Yet, in any international crisis leading to a scramble for resources Japan's diplomatic skills would be fully tested in a manner that its postwar governments have not thus far had to confront.

Economic diplomacy will clearly continue to be a central pillar of Japan's international relations. The nation depends on imported raw materials for its industrial prosperity and some important sectors of its economy are strongly export-oriented. The need to mollify Japan's trading partners as they read of almost continual increases in Japan's current account trade surpluses with other advanced industrial rivals will persist. The problems of success now beset the Japanese economy and its diplomacy. A western Europe battered by high unemployment, low growth and political instability will find it difficult to resist pointing the finger at Japan. Disappointment in Europe and North America at their economic performance will inevitably lead to charges that Japan has broken the rules and reneged on its promises. It will remain an unenviable part of the work of Japanese embassies in other industrialized nations to explain the realities of Japan's trading position and attempt to correct misconceptions.

We ought now to return from the broad generalities of international economics and foreign policy to the more mundane issues behind Japan's current diplomacy. It has already been suggested that Japan's dealing with the United States is the focus of Tokyo's external policies. The two principal bones of contention concern strategic and trade issues that may be best discussed separately, although both share certain common features. We need to assess whether present differences make it increasingly likely that references to Japan as the United States' 'most important single ally' could shift to talk of Washington and Tokyo as 'economic and political adversaries'.

It does not necessarily help to restrict our discussion only to bilateral matters. Japan and the United States may well have divergent views on the nature of the strategic balance in east Asia and the western Pacific that would inevitably colour how each state sees the world. Japan appears to prefer to play down the Soviet military build-up in the region, while the United States has been anxious to instil a less complacent attitude in the minds of Japanese politicians and bureaucrats. This will be difficult to achieve. Not only has Tokyo been reluctant to agree over the extent of the Soviet 'danger' in northeast Asia, it is also burdened by a lengthy Soviet–Japanese agenda. Aside from the perennial issue of the northern islands, this includes the need for Soviet agreement on Japanese fishing in its waters, the interest of Japanese industry in Siberian and Sakhalian development projects and the wish to retain flying rights over Soviet territory to Moscow and points beyond. To put it bluntly, the Soviet Union is a near neighbour of immense military and industrial power, rich in natural resources. Geography and missiles make a formidable combination.

It was, of course, to prevent any possibility of Japan falling under the influence of the Soviet Union that the United States was determined to anchor Tokyo within its camp after the end of the Pacific war. Rumours of any wavering by the United States on the extent of its commitments to Japan inevitably bring into question the entire future of Japanese foreign policy. There have been a number of instances going back to the occupation years when some Japanese felt that the United States might be less than wholeheartedly bound to Japan. Recent public opinion polls suggest that the bulk of the Japanese people are satisfied with the present state of US–Japanese relations but only a small minority appear to be ready to consider closer ties to Washington. The greatest difficulty with such reasoning from an American perspective is that it ignores the deficiencies in the United States' military posture in the Pacific and the growing number of American complaints about the imbalance of the US–Japan relationship. Yet, though there may well be a security gap, little will be done by Japan in the 1980s to fill it. Aside from voicing the familiar charge of 'free-rider' there are few options left to the United States. It needs Japan every bit as much as it assumes Japan needs the United States.

If the likelihood then of the security issue being solved to the satisfaction of the Pentagon is somewhat remote, how may we assess the other running sore? The trade issue is equally unlikely to be resolved in any immediate manner that might bring political returns to an American administration. The trade gap has grown, is growing and will continue to grow. Anger at the extent of Japan's penetration into sectors of the American economy will continue so long as Japanese cars and electrical goods find a ready market. Currently one quarter of all Japanese exports are destined for the United States and, while it is certainly true that Japan's largest source of imports is the United States, most of this trade is accounted for in primary products. Japan imports only a handful of American cars annually. Japanese consumers have no need to purchase personal computers made in the United States. How then can the serious trade disputes between Japan and the United States be resolved? Is it indeed sensible to discuss international economics on a bilateral basis?

It would certainly assist the Japanese case if a global view of Japan's trading position could be introduced into the public debate, but politicians facing re-election can hardly be expected to find their constituents enamoured by the idea. While it may be demonstrable that American consumers have gained by enhanced competition and improved quality brought about by the introduction of Japanese goods, it is also undoubtedly the case that certain American industries have been damaged by Japan's success. Trade associations and trades unions have the political power to resist these developments. The agreement to limit the exportation of Japanese cars to the United States is one important example of Japanese manufacturers being prepared to recognize the dangers of overkill. The reluctance of Japanese farmers to comply with American requests for greatly increased imports of citrus fruits, tobacco and beef is an example of an alternative response.

It is not part of our purpose to ascribe responsibility for these trade disputes but it is important to present rival interpretations. In the popular American view, the United States is on the receiving end of a carefully controlled series of export promotions that are held to be destroying American jobs. (The fact that the State of California, in particular, has received a considerable boost in employment through Japanese investment is invariably overlooked.) The problem is exacerbated by an even firmer belief that the Japanese market has both formal and informal trade restrictions that have conspired to prevent American manufacturers from gaining a fair opportunity to sell their goods within Japan. The prevalence of such views is unlikely to be diminished by periodic official announcements on new measures to expedite Japanese imports. A series of similar much-heralded measures has left considerable doubts as to whether the easing of customs regulations and the removal of non-tariff barriers has in fact occurred. Japanese bureaucrats tend to react to foreign pressure by both pointing out the relatively low level of remaining trade restrictions and simultaneously promising to correct what one must assume to be formidable non-tariff barriers. The seemingly endless saga of the difficulties involved in persuading Japanese organizations to permit the import and purchase of American-made metal baseball bats is but one trivial example of widespread 'buy Japanese' attitudes. While such public behaviour has, of course, its counterparts overseas, it is not easy to explain the low level of finished goods imported by Japan. It is hard to imagine that in all cases there is a superior or cheaper Japanese substitute.

Attempts to redress the trade imbalance will take much more than mass imports of baseball bats and Californian oranges. What presumably is required of the United States is a shift in business attitudes to meet greatly increased Japanese competition. Statistics tell part of the story. The commitment by Japanese companies in establishing local offices in the United States has rarely been matched by an equal American investment of money and manpower into the Japanese market. The track record too of American firms in Japan is hardly comparable to the Japanese triumphs in the United States. The fact that Toyota is one of the three largest car makers in the world is particularly galling to Detroit and the American psyche. Japan exported fewer than 2,000 cars in 1960 to the United States, yet by 1980 it was sending

1,820,000 cars and carving out for itself a large share of the American market. Japanese engineers have also taken on and seemingly defeated the United States in some semiconductor products. (Japan claims to have 70% of the world market for the 64K RAM microchip.) All this has prompted a vast array of American reactions. Some observers have called for a strengthened bureaucracy better organized to fight off the Japanese challenge, while others have preferred to complain at the allegedly improper collusion between Japanese business and government. It is not easy to imagine that the Japanese advantage can be overturned in the 1980s. Japan's advantages, such as a willingness to adopt a long-term view and to cultivate a market without expecting an immediate return on investment, will continue to pay off. Critics who voice doubts about Japan's non-tariff barriers, the undervaluation of the yen and Tokyo's encouragement of export drives to compensate for slack domestic demand may well score debating points but fail to stop the behemoth.

The problems facing American–Japanese relations are formidable. Major differences over Pacific security and a sizeable Japanese current account trade surplus with the United States reckoned to be in excess of $20 billion for 1983 are not solvable in the short term. Changes over what the Japanese government might consider to be a larger, more appropriate defence role and measures to correct the trade imbalance will hardly be overcome in the remainder of this decade. Indeed there are not a few American pessimists who predict little from the Japanese beyond agreement that Tokyo ought to re-define its international responsibilities and an increased trade surplus.

Where then does this leave the two Pacific allies? All alliances are ultimately marriages of convenience and we must assume that the two nations will continue to regard each other as vital trading partners that have equally important stakes in Asian regional stability. It follows therefore that their differences will damage but not ultimately disrupt their friendship. At times when American congressmen are calling for domestic-content legislation and Japanese farmers are resisting American agricultural imports this will appear to be an act of faith. Yet the consequences of any serious break are probably sufficiently dire to induce a cautionary note that may prevent any lasting damage to the international system. We must hope so.

If Japan's relations with the United States are at present under strain, Tokyo's dealings with Moscow can only be described as at their worst since 1945. The causes are many and they tend to more than counterbalance the interests of those Japanese fishermen and businessmen who remain anxious for Soviet co-operation. The historical explanation for Japanese and Soviet wariness is understandable. Imperial Japan fought against Russia on four occasions from the Russo-Japanese war of 1904–5 to the Siberian intervention of 1918–22, the border skirmishes of 1938 and 1939 at Changkufeng and Nomonhan and finally the short seven-day war at the fag end of the Pacific war. The Soviet drive on Japanese troops in Manchuria contributed greatly to Japan's decision to surrender in August 1945 and was seen by the Red army and naval commanders as the wiping of the slate for the defeats of the Russo-Japanese war. Khrushchev pointed out in an interview with the *Asahi Shimbun*'s editor in 1957 that those in Japan who continued to criticize the Soviet Union for abrogating its neutrality pact with Japan in 1945 might care to recall the undeclared attack by Imperial forces on Port Arthur at the start of the Russo-Japanese war.

At the heart of the many differences between Tokyo and Moscow lies the unresolved question of the northern islands. Japanese claims to the islands are based on 19th-century treaties with Russia and arguments that the Soviet Union misunderstood the Potsdam Declaration and San Francisco Treaty. Failure to reach agreement on the fate of the four islands (Habomai, Shikotan, Etorofu and Kunashiri) comprising, in the Soviet view at least, the southernmost part of the Kurile island chain has prevented Japan and the Soviet Union from signing a peace treaty. The decision of Prime Minister Suzuki to designate 7 February as 'northern territories day' and the incorporation of anti-Soviet passages in the annual Defence White Paper are indicative of the government's wish to reinforce public opinion over what most Japanese regard as Soviet intransigence. Statements by Soviet officials, such as the one made by its ambassador to Japan that his nation has no spare territory to give away, have not helped placate Japan. The subject came nearest to possible solution during the peace negotiations held in London and Moscow in 1955–6, but the offer of two of the four islands by Moscow during a confused period of intra-party struggle was rejected by Hatoyama. The eventual normalization of relations between Japan and the Soviet Union occurred in October 1956, when the Japanese government's hopes of gaining a fishing agreement, Soviet approval of Tokyo's admittance to the United Nations and the repatriation of the remaining Japanese internees and prisoners of war held in the Soviet Union were realized. Yet the northern island dispute has dragged on, preventing the conclusion of a formal peace treaty. Prospects for any future settlement of the territorial question are dim.

Broader nationalistic and strategic differences have also contributed to this worsening of Japanese–Soviet relations. Having regained Okinawa in May 1972 from the United States, it was certain that Japanese attention would focus on its irredentist claims to the northern islands and their rich fishing resources. Reports of the construction of Soviet bases on the islands and alleged interference by Soviet ships with Japanese trawlers are grist to the Japanese mill. Were Japan ever to repossess the islands, the strategic balance of the area would immediately shift since Tokyo and Washington might then be able to blockade the Tsugaru strait and bottle up the Soviet Pacific fleet at Vladivostok. Wider factors are also at work to foreclose any possible solution to the territorial deadlock. The Soviet invasion of Afghanistan in 1979 and the imposition of martial law on Poland in 1981 were denounced by the Japanese government, as was the Soviet threat in 1983 to redeploy any SS20 missiles withdrawn from eastern Europe to its Asian borders. The Japanese foreign ministry was only too well aware that the region might end up as the atomic dustbin for an arms control agreement restricted by both superpowers to Europe only. The reality of Soviet power, whether expressed militarily through its blue-water naval build-up, and the shooting down of a Korean Airlines aeroplane in September 1983 off Sakhalin, or politically by its influence on developments in Indochina and Korea, can only weaken the fading calls for Japanese–Soviet co-operation.

If Japanese–Soviet relations appear destined to remain cool, what may be said of Tokyo's contacts with Peking? Is it possible to see here a gradual embrace at the expense of the Soviet Union, drawing on the sentimental and cultural links between Japan and a greater civilization? How permanent should one expect the improvement in Sino-Japanese relations to be? What roles can either pursue independently of the two superpowers with their competing interests in the region?

Our starting point for this brief survey will be Prime Minister Tanaka's visit to Peking in September 1972. He went, to the accompaniment of a fanfare of publicity and impressive opinion polls, to establish diplomatic relations with the People's Republic of China. It was the second act of a 'diplomatic revolution', following closely on the Kissinger–Nixon decision to go to Peking that had supposedly disturbed the Japanese government and set off alarm bells on the merits of the US–Japanese alliance. Yet relations between Japan and China – symbolized by a 'panda boom' among young Japanese – have rarely followed the optimistic path predicted in the months after normalization took place. Japan has been careful not to give offence to the Soviet Union by participating in any triple *entente* between Tokyo, Washington and Peking that might have military overtones. Japan's trading links with Taipei have not been sundered.

Japan's return to diplomatic relations with mainland China did not mean the end of the two-China policy that had characterized its dealings with the rival Chinese regimes during the past thirty years. Japan, for all the American pressure associated with the Yoshida letter (whereby the premier promised to have no truck with Peking) and the consequent April 1952 peace treaty with Nationalist China, had long endeavoured to keep its options open and avoid excessive kowtowing to the United States. This process has continued since the normalization of relations and the eventual signing of a Sino-Japanese treaty of peace and friendship in August 1978. Tokyo has no wish to lose its valuable commercial and financial ties with Taiwan or enter into a tight relationship with either the People's Republic of China or the Soviet Union, since any such action towards one could only antagonize the other. War guilt, appreciation of Chiang Kai-shek's attitude towards occupied Japan (his government renounced its reparation claims) and personal and economic ties with Taiwan had to be balanced after 1952 against those within the LDP and the opposition parties who favoured links with the People's Republic. Although public opinion by 1972 was overwhelmingly in favour of normalizing relations with Peking, 75% of those polled expressed regret at the severance of diplomatic relations with Taiwan. A similar ambivalence has persisted. Japanese doubts as to where China stood in the strategic confrontation between the United States and the Soviet Union have certainly not been clarified as Peking sensed that its freedom to play off the two superpowers against one another had grown by the 1980s.

Japan's own freedom to manoeuvre is clearly more limited. Events since 1952 have already demonstrated where its ultimate objectives lie. Tokyo would like to improve its already amicable contacts with China, to whom it has granted considerable loans and launched teaching programmes as part of its growing cultural diplomacy, and from whom it has expectations of engineering orders and oil-exploration contracts, but this has to be seen within the context of more pressing US–Japanese relations. Although Japan's foreign policy priorities are unlikely to shift, it will press for closer ties to Peking. The Japanese government and its industrial supporters have repeatedly informed the People's Republic that it is eager to assist in China's modernization (Japan is China's largest trading partner) and that it has no desire to build up the SDF to a level that might rekindle earlier Chinese fears. But it is unlikely to be a comfortable re-alignment. Peking may harbour doubts over the strengthening of Japan's economic ties to a developing nation with a host of bureaucratic and industrial difficulties ahead of it and the Chinese furor over the confused 1982 Japanese textbook controversy demonstrates how raw its nerves remain. (The publicity over the incident was generated by false reporting by a section of the Japanese press but it remains the case that bureaucrats continue to check the suitability of classroom texts.)

For the moment it is apparent that Sino-Japanese relations are relatively warm in comparison with the frigidity of Soviet–Japanese contacts, but those engaged with international relations have to bear in mind the future possibilities and potential of a nuclear-armed and industrializing China. A legacy of past estrangement, ideological differences and divergent economic systems might not be easily overcome, despite much public stress on cultural similarities (only a handful of Japanese speak Chinese in reality) and promises to expand joint developmental projects. It would be premature to anticipate any permanent relaxation until the larger regional configurations are clearer.

There are other threats to Japan's security that also require mention. The most important of these concerns the Korean peninsula. Here large military forces with rival superpower sponsors face each other in a divided land. Japan's own relations with South Korea have been uneasy (not surprisingly in the light of Japan's colonial past) and Tokyo has yet to establish diplomatic relations with Pyongyang. The problems of clouding Japanese–South Korean relations are many. The legacy of imperialism has left both the Korean and Japanese publics ill-prepared even now for any substantial meeting of minds (relations were not normalized until 1965) and the future may be equally difficult at times. For the Japanese government, a reduction of tension on the Korean peninsula would be a blessing, but any unilateral moves by the United States (President Carter was persuaded to change his mind over promised troop withdrawals) would be strongly resisted. Japan's economic interests in South Korea are now substantial, though there are frequent complaints from the Korean side over the predatory attitudes of Japanese capitalism and the unwillingness of Tokyo to provide sufficient development assistance to boost further what some Japanese see as a swiftly emerging industrial rival.

Japan and western Europe have not made a success of their postwar relations. The titles of recent versions of these events make it apparent that the story is one of 'misunderstanding' or alternatively 'conflict and co-operation'. Neither the Europeans nor the Japanese ought to be satisfied with what has frequently been a bad-tempered and disappointing series of trade wrangles with little attempt to identify shared interests and values. Why has the situation deteriorated? What suggestions might be welcomed to remove some of the plentiful misperceptions?

European views of Japan in the early postwar days were far from complimentary. Memories of the Pacific war and fears of a repetition of trade practices employed in the 1930s were the backcloth to Japan's re-emergence as an international competitor. European attempts in the 1950s to exclude Japan from GATT were not to be easily forgiven or forgotten by senior Japanese diplomats and trade negotiators later. Undoubtedly these mutual suspicions have left an unfortunate legacy that could be resurrected by politicians and journalists who wished to depict Japan as an unprincipled trader that hid behind its island moat while plotting the death of European machine tools, cars, motorbikes and electronics industries. While the Japanese knowledge of even the larger members of the European Community (EC) is not always as substantial as some apologists would maintain, it is undoubtedly greater than that held by many Europeans of Japan. Any British ambassador to Tokyo must find it difficult to explain to his hosts how a majority of his countrymen apparently regard Japan as an appendage of China, peopled by low-wage earners whose government has long possessed nuclear weapons. Image here equals unreality.

A collective European image of Japan today can only be guessed at. It might incorporate super-express trains, the death of Mishima Yukio, the novel *Shogun*, Mount Fuji, smog in Tokyo, the phrases 'economic animals' and 'rabbit hutches', Toyota cars and the Siam–Burma railway. It is largely a combination of technological accomplishment, doubts over the price the Japanese people have had to pay for their economic success and snippets of history. If we add Pearl Harbor, the bomber 'Enola Gay' that destroyed Hiroshima, General MacArthur's direction of the occupation and memories of the Atsugi and Yokosuka bases to our list we have perhaps a comparable American picture. In both cases the image is one of economic tensions and respect underpinned by earlier military confrontations. The forcible opening of Japan by the West in the 19th century and later disadvantageous trading and immigration arrangements imposed on Tokyo are quite forgotten. The fact too that Tokyo was already the largest city in the world by the 18th century and that Japan clearly possessed a considerable pool of talent on which to draw in its later efforts to modernize at speed are also overlooked when accounting for the rise of Japan.

The United States and western Europe, however, have very different approaches towards improving their relations with Japan. At present the United States sees its ties with Japan as possessing a wider dimension than those between the EC and Japan. President Reagan's visit to Japan in November 1983 was intended to demonstrate to the Japanese people the importance that Washington places on Tokyo as a 'global partner'. This hands-across-the-Pacific attitude is in sharp contrast to the strained Japan–Europe links. Headlines over the number of video tape-recorders Japan may be permitted to export to the EC contrast poorly with an American president appearing before the Japanese Diet to deliver a speech that ignored the bitterness of the past in order to concentrate the better on the future. Reports in the same year that the Japanese government had been rebuffed by France over the possibility of establishing a more permanent forum to discuss strategic and political issues of concern to Europe (through NATO) and Japan, may be evidence of use to those who wish to play down the European factor in Japanese foreign policy formulation. The lack of a unified EC approach to Japanese questions only re-inforces such tendencies and permits Japan quite legitimately to play one European state off against another.

Attempts to widen EC–Japanese contacts through increased cultural and personal visits are equally unpromising at the present, since Europeans possess neither sufficient interest nor capital to correct the multitude of howlers in circulation. Foreign journalists in Tokyo cannot always help to rectify the situation. They are obliged to file almost incessant economic stories that concentrate on the problems of simplifying import procedures or the latest monthly export statistics but largely ignore Japanese political or social issues. Certainly there is considerable respect for Japanese products but as yet little awareness of how Japanese factories operate or what impact Japan aspires to have on the wider world. Even a congenital optimist would have cause to ponder if he were to survey current EC–Japan ties. The first priority undoubtedly is to improve the strained economic links, but until the European economies begin to emerge from their present battered condition all one can wish for is that the situation will not deteriorate further. Only after the economic dimension has been repaired should one expect progress over broader political and cultural questions.

The language gap between Japan and the rest of the world is unlikely to be bridged. The drawbacks of an education system that stresses abstruse grammatical points but neglects to attend to spoken English, and the scarcity of Japanese-speakers in the West have produced what has been aptly termed a Himalayan barrier to understanding. The only recourse would seem to be through greater use of translations. Purists would prefer to see improvements made in Japan's foreign language training methods and encouragement for Western students to persevere, but neither state of affairs is probable. Most Western readers interested in Japan will continue to rely on translations for their appreciation of the Japanese novel and subtitles for their enjoyment of the Japanese cinema. It may be second best, but then how many people in Britain or the United States read Kafka or Dostoyevsky in the original? The onus will remain on the skilled specialists to provide an accurate account for the large Japanese audience interested in Western thought and behaviour and the much smaller Western group prepared to look at a culture that remains very much on the fringes of most school and university curricula.

What is the current Japanese world view? Where does it place the United States and western Europe? What images do the Japanese people hold of the non-Western world? In Japanese eyes the parts of the world that count are limited. Historically the three main models for influencing Japanese institutions and behaviour have been China, 19th-century Europe and, since 1945, the United States. The rest of the world may have considerable economic importance to Japan but this has not always led to any great understanding. The photographs of the heads of state and government taken after the annual advanced nations summit best characterize Japan's progress and enhanced self-esteem. The Japanese premier has gradually moved from hanging around on the very edge of the group portrait to being one of the central figures. This recognition by other Western states is what Japan is after. It wishes to see itself and be seen by others as a power worthy of respect. Prime Minister Nakasone was able to stress Japan's improved status by receiving the German chancellor, the United States' president and the secretary-general of the Chinese Communist Party as official guests to Tokyo in the autumn of 1983. Cynics were quick to point out that such events carefully coincided with the forthcoming general election, but this need not detract from the undoubted improvement accorded Japan on the world stage.

The process is not, of course, complete. It is not even certain that Japan's future will lie in greater internationalism. There are, as we have seen, powerful domestic voices which would decry military build-ups or greater aid contributions; there are also other states that might oppose any strengthening of Japan's position. Tokyo, for example, would meet with massive resistance if it seriously campaigned for a permanent seat on the United Nations' Security Council. In 1978 it was humiliated by losing to Bangladesh in the battle to gain a two-year term as the Asian Security Council representative. Likewise, Nagoya had to suffer the indignity of seeing the 1988 Olympic games be awarded to Seoul. Friendships can be fragile and Japan has few states it can rely on. It may have to work harder to gain Asian and Pacific co-operation. A greater sensitivity over its commercial practices and social behaviour might help. More technological assistance to ASEAN states (Malaysia, Singapore, Indonesia, Thailand, the Philippines and Brunei) and fewer all-male group tours to Bangkok and Manila would not go amiss.

'Japan is not an immigrant country.' This recent statement by the director of the Foreign Ministry's division of refugee affairs is a frank and somewhat disappointing commentary on Japanese attitudes towards the rest of the world. Whether the subject is governmental and public resistance to Vietnamese 'boat people', the minuscule interest in support of Amnesty International or opinion polls depicting popular xenophobia, similar wariness emerges. Whatever the historical explanations for such isolationism it is, if only for reasons of Realpolitik, hardly in Japan's interest to perpetuate these attitudes. What might be done to rectify the situation? Or is it sufficient for Japan's dealings with the rest of the world to be restricted to a handful of civil servants and employees of the major trading companies?

We must admit that efforts have been made in the past decade to come to grips with some of the problems. The media and a few politicians have spoken of 'internationalizing' Japan, though the phrase risks being overworked as a substitute for any real action. Government funds have been employed by the Japan Foundation to project a picture of Japan different from the usual diet of balance of payment surpluses, and private industrial foundations have been generous in their support of a few select institutions overseas. Domestic universities and research centres have also been created in an attempt to encourage greater consciousness of the external world. Yet the problems to be surmounted are not solvable merely by such measures, laudable though these efforts may be.

Not much can be done about Japan's history, though deletion from its textbooks of the euphemisms used to describe Japanese aggression in Asia would help, and nothing to alter its geography, but government initiatives might be tried to modify public attitudes. Language instruction in schools could be sharpened up, gestures such as relaxing the nationality laws might be introduced and more attention paid to Japanese aid programmes. None of this is likely to make an instant impression, but it might be received as evidence of a gradual change of heart by overseas audiences. The Japanese picture of the rest of the world unfortunately is a severely hierarchical one that permits little recognition of less developed Asian or African states. It usually accepts North America and western Europe as ageing but respected prize-winners and condemns the remainder of the world to limbo. Given the usual propensities for democracies and their elected representatives to stress bread and butter issues unless facing an imminent threat to their security, it would (once again) be unwise to expect any immediate changes. Japan is likely to remain inward-looking, in keeping with its belief that charity begins and ends at home. The social costs to overseas communities of Japanese exporting prowess are and will be frequently ignored by a public that feels its trade rivals must pull up their socks if they want to remain competitive. Foreign relations will probably still be largely a matter of economic diplomacy. If no longer quite the silent power of a generation ago, Japan will persist in keeping its head down. Any increase in Japan's international stock will be gradual.

Discussion of 'Japan's new world role' is possibly premature. Academics and analysts may be jumping the gun when they talk repeatedly of Japan's political and economic responsibilities in a changing international system. Often the domestic context of Japanese politics is glossed over too rapidly as the commentator leaps to present his personal prescription for how Japan ought to behave in a multi-polar world. There is an air of unreality behind parts of the debate, since the evidence suggests that the Japanese public is decidedly wary of much of this appeal to its pocket and conscience. Opinion polls and editorials repeat that Japan is hesitant over expanding its defence capabilities, despite what it sees as an increase in foreign threats to its territory. The Soviet Union is regarded as an unfriendly neighbour by some Japanese (perhaps a third) but a majority of the public has long doubted whether the United States would protect it in an emergency. The US–Japan

Security Treaty takes on a different hue when seen from the perspective of a public that remains sceptical of the value of this link if put to the test. It is improbable that any Japanese government in the foreseeable future would greatly increase defence spending much beyond 1% of GNP. The suggestion that Japanese industry needs to encourage re-armanent to fill its order books is implausible.

How then is Japan to provide the means for an enlarged international role? The answer rests on one's assessment of likely Japanese political and bureaucratic responses to the counter-forces of domestic opinion and American appeals. The entire subject has to be conjectural and any guess must be prefaced by acknowledgement of one's ignorance. It may be thought pessimistic by some, but the prospect of Japan taking an active role in the defence of sealanes or providing non-military assistance to United Nations peace-keeping forces appears remote. A pragmatic people see little benefit to be gained by contributing to such uncertain ventures. It would take considerable evidence from unfavourable events in east Asia to shift public opinion. The shooting down by the Soviet Union of a KAL aeroplane in 1983 was used by the government to justify its existing military expenditure, rather than as a timely opportunity to add to predetermined appropriations. Reminders of Soviet power might be employed successfully by some as confirmation of the wisdom of retaining a low profile rather than as testimony to support greater militarism.

5

Social change and continuity

Our sketch of contemporary Japanese politics, economics and international relations may have provided some pointers to Japan's present identity, social structure and values. For all the changes since the Pacific war Japan remains a conservative, bourgeois and cautious nation intent on retaining the modified institutions that have served it well since the disasters of militarism seemingly wiped out the handiwork of the previous three generations. We shall first look briefly at Japanese self-perceptions.

No other major industrial society has anything approaching the racial homogeneity of Japan. The largest minority group is the Burakumin composed of the descendants of outcasts with occupations such as butchers, shoe-makers and junk collectors. Prejudice against the more than two million Burakumin is strong and persistent. The only other sizeable minorities are of Korean and Chinese origin – the number of North American and European residents is minuscule. This factor, which has been aided and abetted by the immigration policies of the Japanese government, has contributed to a large degree to the uniformity in Japanese social behaviour. History and geographic isolation have been combined with this racial unity to fuel a strong sense of national identity. It is not and will not become necessary in the future for the Japanese to wonder excessively over what constitutes their national character. It is certainly true that the subject holds a fascination for the public but this pursuit may have an element of narcissism attached to it. Countless articles and books have been produced which analyse the uniqueness of the Japanese people. The readers generally believed this before they bought the texts that said what they already knew but wanted to hear again.

What is Japanese man? How does he define himself? At the first level, a Japanese is someone born of two Japanese parents. Citizenship is acquired through a blood relationship that some feel ought to be rethought in Japan's present nationality laws. As parts of them stand today it is difficult not to hear echoes of the past overriding more recent claims that the state has aspirations to 'internationalism'. Japanese women married to non-Japanese cannot yet pass on their citizenship to their children. Since Japan signed the United Nations' female anti-discrimination convention in 1979 it would appear that change may be in the offing. The likely outcome is for the Diet to pass a bill granting children of non-Japanese fathers and Japanese mothers the right to dual citizenship until they come of age at 20, when they will have to choose which nationality to retain. To be Japanese often also implies a strong attachment to the nation and to its successes. Any immediate postwar feelings of racial inferiority have long since disappeared. By the late 1960s, pollsters discovered that very few Japanese still persisted in any deference to the West, while nearly 50% expressed a sense of superiority. Nationalism is strong. It has played a major role in motivating Japan's recovery and is never too far from the surface when accounts are made of the nation's fall and subsequent rise. Other attributes which may make up the Japanese national character – if such a composite picture can be said to have much value – might include a professed strong sense of family, a very considerable attachment to one's work-place, little sense of religion and perhaps an overwillingness to conform when weighing up possible courses of action. Family pressures on such critical occasions as, for example, the choice of spouse can be intense.

Japan is an overwhelmingly urban society where the bulk of the people are crammed into the narrow coastal belt between Tokyo and Hiroshima. Space is at a premium. Social behaviour under such circumstances probably reflects the need to avoid excessive confrontation with one's neighbours and colleagues. Through past history and present necessity Japanese society may have placed greatest stress on co-operative group activity at the expense of individual endeavour. Consciousness of hierarchy and loyalty to the family, work-place and nation may take precedence over equality and independence.

The encouragement to conform to group norms is presumably drawn from Japan's agrarian experience. Until recently Japan was largely a rural society where the basic social units were the family and village. Sociologists and anthropologists have suggested that parts of the intended village structure have been transferred onto Japan's modern industrial society. Loyalty to one's own small work-group and its supervisor have parallels with the control that a father or landlord might possess. In both cases the safest course of action may be to conform and identify oneself closely with the group and its fate, thereby gaining protection for oneself and the prospect of promotion with others if the company or one's particular section prospers. This may go some way to explain the factionalism of Japanese political, bureaucratic and industrial circles and also the *esprit de corps* of rival groupings within organizations. Dependence – some might claim overreliance – on the group's leader may be the consequence of the persistence into adulthood of common childhood attitudes. The giving of presents to one's professor or manager at mid-summer and the end of the year emphasizes this vertical relationship and implies a request for goodwill, in the tradition of the peasant entreating with his landlord for protection.

By European standards Japan is not quite the small nation that its citizens are intent on projecting overseas, since it is larger than either Britain or West Germany. In comparison with the United States, of course, it appears in a very different light, though even then if superimposed on a map it stretches from Vermont to the Bay of Mexico. What appears difficult to explain is the relative ease with which this vast shift of population from rural to urban Japan has been carried out.

Today's Japan is an urban society based increasingly on the nuclear family. The small size of city accommodation and the mass migration from the countryside to the cities are two factors that are making it less common for grandparents to live with their eldest son and his family. (Japan's population density is higher than any European nation's but below that of Korea and Taiwan.) There are frequent complaints that today's metropolitan generation is suffering from anomie and would wish to return to the less frantic pace of the semi-rural towns, if not the monotony of village life, but the dislocations and neuroses have not produced any great retreat to the country areas. The Japanese people retain a strong sentimental attachment to their home-towns but rarely go back more than once or twice a year for the summer festival and the longer new year holidays. Urban life undoubtedly has its frustrations and inconveniences, centred on the scarcity and price of housing and the virtual necessity for office workers to commute long distances if they are ever to secure a house or apartment of their own in one of the continually expanding suburbs. Housing is grossly expensive. This is caused , inevitably, by the high price of land and the reluctance of those fortunate enough to possess plots in the remaining fringe areas to put their land on the market. Home ownership remains, however, the aspiration of many Japanese for which they are prepared to mortgage their pension rights if necessary.

For many Japanese husbands the work-place takes precedence over the family. The small group comprising one's colleagues within a particular department has a very considerable importance for white-collar workers. One's identity is partially formed through membership of this close-knit group. Salarymen expect to be asked to stay late in the office if the group is under pressure. Evenings are often spent in neighbouring bars in the company of one's work-mates. This inevitably weakens family life. Considerable numbers of Japanese children rarely have dinner with their parents. Even at the weekend (a term which will require definition later) fathers may absent themselves to show a foreign visitor around or to play golf with customers or colleagues.

The company or factory is the focus for the lives of many Japanese. It is not solely that the salaryman puts in long hours there, but he is committed to his work-place in a manner quite distinct from some European or North American behaviour. The employee will almost certainly have joined his company immediately after graduation from university on the understanding that he will devote himself to his particular company for the remainder of his working life. It is rare indeed to resign from one company to join another. Once a worker for Matsushita, always a worker for Matsushita. Having obtained employment with a large or medium-sized company, a young graduate can expect to receive extensive training in management within the organization and at least the prospect of further education overseas or a temporary transfer to an Asian or American subsidiary. He – careers for women are regarded as disruptive to one's own company hierarchy and likely to create friction with firms with which one has business dealings – is on a slowly moving escalator. Obviously not everyone will reach a position of great responsibility within the enterprise but most graduates have the opportunity to progress at least to the foothills.

It may be folly to talk of *the* Japanese company, but certain characteristics appear to be sufficiently widely shared among the larger enterprises to permit an abstract picture. Aside from standard recruitment practices, whereby new employees commence their careers as part of an annual intake every April amidst considerable ceremony and encouragement from the senior management, companies endeavour to provide 'lifetime employment' and remuneration based on a combination of years of service and job responsibility. They will also attempt to assist over housing for employees (hostels for bachelors and apartments in company compounds for younger married couples) and offer a large number of fringe benefits. Both the company and its employee have made, in effect, an arrangement that asks more of each side than might be normally expected in the West. The ideal may not apply as frequently as the more rhapsodical accounts would have us believe, but talented managers are not easily enticed away or the less than competent immediately dismissed. Semi-annual bonuses do reflect the company's past sales performance. Enterprises wish to be seen as a 'family' and do make efforts to live up to their responsibilities. Mass sackings because of a sudden downturn in business are very much a measure of last resort. Redeployment elsewhere within the corporation or early retirement – suitably sweetened – would be the norm.

Most of the features in our account apply only to the graduate entrants within the larger Japanese companies. The conditions under which others work can be far less pleasant: blue-collar workers, those employed in subsidiary firms and the temporary staff get a rawer deal. These categories gain fewer benefits from their employer and are regarded as no more than adjuncts to the company for whom they may be working. Wages in smaller companies are lower, working conditions are less pleasant and safe, bonuses can be minimal and job security non-existent. Yet, Japan, as may be recalled from our chapter on its economic growth, remains a nation of small businesses and backstreet factories. Dualism lives. Here younger workers are much more likely to vote with their feet and move to another firm that promises higher wages and more overtime. The attempts to provide a company network that might bind the employee to his enterprise are necessarily weaker since owners have no spare funds for such luxuries. Bankruptcy fears rather than plans for company-organized tours (males only) to Bangkok occupy the lives of small bosses.

Yet, despite greater job mobility and a considerably reduced wage-packet in smaller companies, much of the same attitude towards work exists throughout the Japanese economy. Society accepts that work is an activity that requires the giving of one's best, whether one is a middle manager in the Tokyo head office wearing pinstripes and the company badge in one's lapel or a junior worker on the assembly line in the sub-urban factory wearing the alternative uniform of grey battledress. Although packed coffee shops and pinball arcades may suggest otherwise, one's workplace is something that helps define onself ('I work for Sony, he's from Matsushita') and the activity is assumed to be socially valuable. Management under such circumstances is different, though not necessarily any easier than that in the West. Those in authority may well face fewer direct challenges to their decisions but it is assumed by their subordinates that efforts will be made to involve the entire group in the pursuit of the company's objectives. Emotional ties may be stronger and the hours spent in gaining this trust and co-operation can be long. Some may claim that the consultation process has an element of fraud behind it, since the company can ultimately insist on getting its own way, but few managers worth their salt would wish to resort to such heavy-handed tactics. Besides, a well motivated work-force is likely to identify more closely with the company and see the sales targets and production control data as their shared goal with the enterprise. A vertical society that pits one's own company against rival firms has less time for class warfare.

To the Western reader the Japanese company must appear at first glance to be a strange bird. Management by approximate consensus, with age greatly influencing promotion until comparatively early retirement (often at 55 but gradually being extended to 58 or 60) forces one to leave is clearly not the manner in which most European firms are accustomed to operating. The trend in the West is for reductions in the working week, longer holidays and for pressure to rethink the retirement system. In Japan the reverse has taken place. The work week remains longer than in parts of Europe, holidays are short and acceptance of large amounts of unpaid overtime by all ranks above quite junior white-collar workers is common. It also makes much heavier social demands on employees. Such a system has little built-in countervailing power. Trades unions are generally weak and often inhibited by being company-based organizations. (It is not unknown for senior managers to have served in their earlier days with the company union.) Ultimately what saves the system from tyranny is the Japanese social climate that conditions both workers and management over equitable behaviour and the continuing successes of the economy. Managers generally appreciate how far they can press their rulings, while the postwar booms have made it easier to negotiate wage settlements. Labour disputes are rare outside the somewhat ritualistic spring bargaining season, when white-gloved stationmasters on JNR can be seen tearing down posters the moment unionists deface state property. Strikes do occur on occasion, but most of the animosity of the occupation period when unions challenged management quite openly has disappeared. Yet it was probably the lessons drawn by companies from the early postwar bitterness that gained wider acceptance of 'permanent employment' and a wage related to the individual's family responsibilities. Public memories may have long faded of the days when Toyota was racked by a lengthy labour dispute in 1950 that nearly brought the company to its knees, but the affair was taken to heart by the management.

Japanese education remains a subject of considerable domestic political debate. It has also been of interest to overseas audiences and readers, as the international reporting of the 1982 textbook issue and the student events of the 1960s demonstrated. Recent American awareness of the problems of public education has led also to increasingly favourable comparisons between the Japanese educational system and those of its industrial competitors. Is such praise warranted? What are the strengths and weaknesses of Japanese education?

The subject is controversial. Writing 20 years ago, one British student of Japanese society went so far as to claim that 'perhaps no other educational system in the world is so continuously and so earnestly fought over'. If tempers have cooled in the intervening period, it remains the case that every year the Japanese teachers' union (Nikkyoso) has to hold its annual conference under close police protection to prevent mobs of ultra-rightists from physical disruption and attempting to deploy loudhailers to drown out all speakers. Perhaps today, however, the political issues – governmental textbook approval excepted – have decreased as attention has focused on the drawbacks of excessive pressure on university entrance examinees and the heavy out-of-school studying that forms a prominent part of the regime of even junior high school members.

A decent education is crucial to the life chances of young Japanese. Since Japan can be loosely defined as a meritocracy where one's first job after graduation is often one's only one, many Japanese are eager to compete for the undoubted advantages that entry into a prestigious university can bring in terms of career and even marriage prospects. Parental wishes for their sons to aspire to a top-ranking university are inculcated from an early age. Admittance to a good high school is a virtual *sine qua non* for future success, since without competent teachers and a competitive atmosphere only the exceptional pupil will be able to make it. The failure rate for entrance to Tokyo or Kyoto National Universities is inevitably very high, but it does not deter the ambitious from attempting to reach the pinnacle. Only a few can succeed, while the remainder either try again in the following year or make do with their second or third preferences in a pecking order that students and employers alike recognize. Parallels with the rankings made in Anglo-Saxon academic circles are close.

Like it or not (and many on the right do not), Japanese postwar education has found it hard to shrug off its occupation legacy. The outward form of the American educational reforms has remained largely intact. It is true that the control of education has shifted somewhat but the organization of public education was never likely to move far from the control of the Ministry of Education (Monbusho), even in the heady days of decentralization. The shorthand method to describe the postwar reforms is to note that a unified 6–3–3–4 structure defines the new lengths of education available to pupils from elementary school, commencing at six years of age, to junior high school, commencing at 12 and completed at 15, through to three years of high school education and then, for a minority even today, on finally to a four-year university course. Prewar education had only been compulsory up to the completion of elementary school at the age of 12; thereafter the pyramid had rapidly narrowed with universities very much an élitist affair admitting few women students.

The United States' advisers and the GHQ staff in the Civil Information and Education section aimed to democratize both the content and administration of public education. The reformers probably had better luck with their first goal. If the Japan of the 1930s and 1940s had regarded education as a tool in the service of the state, the occupation authorities attempted to introduce less nationalistic values and promote a greater sense of individualism and respect for democratic values. Teachers, like other groups in Japanese society, were eager to sail with the new breeze and quickly saw their role as preventing any back-sliding by the Japanese establishment. Education became something of a battlefield. This did not prevent it from attempting to cater for an enormous upsurge in demand for instruction that might assist in finding one a niche in what by the 1960s had become an affluent society. More and more pupils elected to stay on longer at school in order better to compete for a more prosperous future.

The results have not been entirely happy. Public high school education can be of a high standard (mathematics, for example, is a subject at which Japanese excel in international merit tables), but the goal appears to be more often the passing of examinations than the development of personal abilities and a critical spirit. Universities, for their part, expanded their student enrolments far faster than they were able to provide additions to their faculty or facilities. Horror stories of staff reduced to employing microphones to enable themselves to be heard in vast auditoriums abound. Students under such circumstances are fortunate to be on more than nodding acquaintance with their professors. Such conditions played an important part in student dissatisfaction during the 1960s and have only been partially repaired in the years since. Certainly the government has increased the share of national resources devoted to education in both the public and private sectors, but the discrepancies in budgetary allocation and teaching staff between a select national university and a provincial private college can be vast.

Student attitudes towards their education have inevitably varied, but there is undoubtedly a persistent feeling that university life may provide a moratorium on overtaxing one's intellect. It is as if the heavy pressures to gain admittance to a reputable university and the knowledge that in four years one will have to get back into harness and slog away in a trading company or bank combine to encourage the widespread notion that university life should be a pleasant interlude.

The Japanese public's sense of unease at some features of its educational structure has grown as the competition for the better high schools and universities has intensified. All political parties in the December 1983 general election produced their pet solutions for the problems of education. Yet, as with the malaise over political funding, part of the blame must be attributed to parents who simultaneously complain of the 'examination hell' that their offspring are subjected to and yet insist on ensuring that their children attend cramming schools (*juku*) and tolerate the rote learning essential for passing the entrance examinations. The system may be absurd but the present is apparently not the moment to jeopardize one's son's future. The public is well aware of the glittering prizes that can await the successful Tokyo University entrant. No wonder the examination results for national universities are carefully scrutinized by parents, teachers and personnel managers. No wonder too that the live television broadcasts announcing the university entrance results are sponsored by the crammers.

Japanese education has remained largely centralized and uniform. The proverbial 19th-century French minister of education who could reputedly sit at his desk and know what his teachers were all up to at any given moment would feel at home if transported to contemporary Japan. (National schemes for education in Meiji Japan were based on French models.) It is true that there have been a number of experimental schools and private initiatives, but these have tended to be ignored in the fight to attain the treasured university place. This goal has left education less egalitarian as middle-class parents have increasingly been prepared to fund private schools where the tuition is felt to be better geared to this end. The result can be seen in the background of successful Tokyo University entrants. The scramble has now reached even the kindergarten level. Prosperous families work hard at developing contacts that might assist their children in starting off on the right foot at the appropriate elementary school and then continuing along the same conveyor belt. Education – a sphere of family life usually the exclusive responsibility of Japanese mothers – is too important a business to be left to chance.

If the press is to be believed, the spectre of an ageing population is haunting Japan. Prophets of doom are eager to point out that Japan's population profile is rapidly changing as grandparents live longer and their sons and grandsons have fewer children. Some of this talk needs to be put in perspective. It is true that Japanese life expectancy is the highest on earth and there will be increased pressure on health services and pension schemes by 2000. It is also a fact that the gradual ageing of Japan will have uncomfortable consequences for Japanese industry and the entire social fabric. Yet Japan's present population is still a relatively young one, with only 9% of its people over 65 years of age in comparison with 14% in Britain and 15% in West Germany. Demographers contend that by the end of the first quarter of the 21st century Japan may have caught up with and perhaps surpassed Europe in its share of retirees, but these can be no more than intelligent guesses based on projections into the future of current trends that have necessarily discounted the possibility of upward changes in the birth rate. It might be better to keep an open mind on all this; even actuaries have been known to nod.

What is already apparent is that the structure of Japan's workforce must change and that some further weakening of family ties is likely as more elderly people live apart from their relatives. Japanese enterprises are facing these issues by asking some of their employees to retire early and by taking on more part-time workers in an attempt to control the escalation in their costs which inevitably follows from a salary system that has a strong bias towards seniority and corresponding annual wage increases. The government for its part would dearly like to raise the age at which national pensions are payable (from 60 to 65), but its suggestions on that score have been howled down by the public. At the moment both its statisticians and private industry's managers are uncertain how to proceed. It is likely that most firms will gradually agree to a higher retirement age for its more competent employees, while the government will be forced to raise pension and welfare contributions as the portion of the population nearing retirement age increases. No cabinet likes to increase taxes but, given the size of Japan's existing government deficit, it might be better to face the age problem sooner rather than later. The necessary funding for a greying society cannot be postponed indefinitely.

The bill for providing pension and medical care to a burgeoning portion of the Japanese people is not yet in. The present social security system is a complex amalgam of state and private components with low costs and high benefits in relation to national income. Obviously this will have to change as the demands on the pension funds escalate and the health burden grows, although attempts to increase contributions to governmental medical services have been resented by the public. It also dislikes the system whereby general practitioners appear on occasion to overcharge their patients, knowing that the insurance schemes will take care of inflated receipts. Reforms are needed but face powerful resistance from pressure groups. What is probably clear is that the social strains associated with an ageing population will be less than in western Europe. Far fewer Japanese grandparents are likely to be shunted off into old people's homes or geriatric ghettos on the warmer Pacific coast. Family obligations are still strong; age can have its rewards. It would raise few eyebrows if, for example, the LDP were to elect a new party president in his seventies rather than gamble with a younger figure in his fifties. Some distinguished industrial figures have been known to remain in harness into their eighties. Gerontocracy may not rule, but it can still subtly influence events from the sidelines.

Important economic and political change confronts today's Japan. Pessimists would claim that this is likely to create major tensions for the future, yet it might be safer to assume that these forces will not seriously disrupt the existing social structure. Identity shifts are taking place and the last decade has witnessed what has been called an 'introspection boom', as readers eagerly bought up accounts that redefined their nation, but this need not imply accommodation will be impossible. A survey of some of the issues in the domestic sphere and with regard to foreign policy might be useful.

Much attention has been focused on the young. Youth is better educated (or at least stays on longer at school and university) but it can hardly be said to have rejected conservative values. Competition in high schools for the glittering prizes that admittance to a decent university can bring has not slackened off. The mushrooming of *juku* and the use of private tutors, deplorable as it may be for the very young, is testimony to the achievement orientation of many. The pressures on middle- and high-school students have led many to espouse the cause of educational reform. Nakasone said it was one of his main objectives for 1984, not least because much of the increasing amount of juvenile delinquency has been attributed to educational factors. Vandalism and assaults are attributed to those who do less well in school. The issue of delinquency gets reams of attention in the press and on television, but it often appears relatively mild in comparison with the behaviour of teenagers in some European and American cities. Certainly by the time most students reach university there does not appear to be much anger in evidence. The LDP is reputed to be the most popular political party on many campuses. Surveys of Japanese figures whom students claim to admire are topped by Tanaka Kakuei. No doubt this is partly tongue-in-cheek, but the popularity of self-made men such as Tanaka and Matsushita Konosuke, the founder of the electronics empire, is very much in keeping with the views of the general public. Japanese youth has one great advantage over its Western counterparts. Employment opportunities have remained good during a period that is seeing the highest European dole figures since the 1930s. This has contributed to the present retreat to privatism and political apathy. Having to hold down a job, while conforming to most family and company norms, means that youth is hardly about to change the status quo.

The problems of education are inevitably linked to the reconsideration of the role of women in Japanese society. Women take their twin tasks of mother and housewife seriously, but with the size of families decreasing and the time necessary to maintain a small apartment or house diminishing many wish to find other outlets as their families grow up. Japanese men have not been particularly sympathetic. Single women can find jobs, though not often careers, but the choices for married women when they try to rejoin the labour force are restricted. The entire structure of companies would have to be rethought if women were to be regarded as possessing equal rights. Men would (and do) resist supervision by women. No Japanese bank has appointed a female branch manager. The LDP selected only one woman to run in the December 1983 election and, with the exception of the JCP, the other parties were equally timid. No solution for a change of this magnitude in what women might wish to do with their lives is yet likely. It would take at least a generation for women to make any substantial inroads into the company hierarchies, assuming some were able to get a foot on to the career escalator.

Within the existing family the great attention that mothers give their offspring has both had an immensely beneficial influence on the children's development and created psychological difficulties. Fathers, as we have seen, often leave the responsibility of bringing up children to wives. This may create too strong a bond between the mother and her young, which she may consciously or unconsciously promote. The result has been a legacy of overdependence for some, which leaves the child disappointed when his or her wishes and desire for affection are responded to less frequently or less intently later.

One commonly shared source of pride for many Japanese has been the growth of its economy. So accustomed has the public become to substantial annual increases in Gross Domestic Product that the press refers to predictions of 4% growth for the mid 1980s as 'low'. Slight it may be to those who can recall the double-digit years, but when most advanced industrial nations are only now emerging from the worst period of economic depression since the 1930s the adjective is a comment on current Japanese expectations. Japanese economic success has led, not surprisingly, to greater self-confidence in its leaders and people. It has also presented something of a dilemma for those concerned with Japan's future. Since the West can hardly be held up any longer as a model to be emulated, alternative goals have had to be proposed. These, it should be noted, are not put forward as alternatives to growth but rather as supplements to it. Prime Minister Nakasone could, therefore, in the course of his election campaign in December 1983 claim that he was 'trying to turn Japan into a country of peace and politics and culture – an international state'. The reference to culture, by which he presumably meant most forms of leisure activity from the cultivation of sports and hobbies to more serious intellectual endeavours, was a theme that the premier had used frequently in policy statements to the Diet. It was based on the premise of continued economic achievement. Nakasone's call at the beginning of his first term in office for 'a country of resilient culture and leisure' was intended to increase communitarianism and re-evaluate the postwar reforms, while warning the public that 'even though Japan may be said to be better off than most countries, we face immediate problems in the economy'. No room for slackers was the message. The subject of Japanese identity is one dear to the hearts of many Japanese. It is likely to remain a most imprecise quest, with opportunities for seemingly endless discussion on where Japan is and where it ought to be going. Some would argue that Japan's postwar history might be seen as an attempt to reconsider where the nation went wrong and how it might better behave with new values. The more sceptical observer might well respond to this type of argument by noting how little Japan had changed in reality. The debate is certain to continue. We might draw up a rough balance sheet to assess the relative strengths of the forces of change and the counter-pressure of continuity.

Our account of Japan's experience from 1945 to 1983 has suggested that much of the forced change imposed on Japan during the occupation years has persisted. Parts have undoubtedly been rejected and other portions modified better to fit Japanese circumstances, but large sections of the occupation's handiwork still exist. Should retired officials from the United States' Government Section or the Labour Division of SCAP revisit Japan they would find little difficulty in recognizing parts of their legacy.

There may well have been prewar precedents for parliamentary democracy or trades unionism, but the impetus from the Allies to strengthen what by 1945 were no more than latent elements in a wartime polity based on quite separate values should not be forgotten. Similarly the constitutional provisions with respect to Japan's defence and foreign policies have not been scrapped. Japan today can hardly be described as a military threat to the security of the Pacific. If its foreign policy appears weak-kneed we might remind ourselves that it has few sanctions that it can impose in order to gain its objectives. Of how many nation-states now in the United Nations can it be said that they have not fired a shot in anger since 1945? Precious few. The belief that Japan ought to continue to behave in accordance with the 1947 constitution is strong. Public opinion can be relied on for the remainder of the 1980s and probably beyond to oppose measures that some ministers might wish to implement to increase substantially. Japan's defence capabilities. This may not be popular with the Pentagon but it will be greeted with relief in those areas of Asia that recall the Japanese wartime occupiers.

Tokyo, however, can be rebuked for not breaking out of its chrysalis to approach the rest of the world except largely on the economic level. Japan's perceptions may be changing but until the evidence of this is apparent judgment has to be reserved on any real change of heart. The globe is still seen as a market for Japanese finished goods and a source of raw materials. This is a continuation of prewar industrial policy. 'Export or Die' and 'Buy Japanese' are unstated slogans deeply embedded in the popular consciousness. Foreign manufactured goods rarely make a dent in Japan's balance of trade surplus. Europeans, no doubt, ought to try harder, but Japanese spokesmen have a habit of gliding over their government's earlier trade policies that aided the growth of nascent industries. It would be surprising if Japan's bureaucrats and industrialists were readily to alter their instinctive response to promote exports when the domestic economy faces a mild recession. There is yet to be much action, as opposed to reaction, to overseas threats of protectionism, that takes note of the consequences of trading successes. At present the government encourages export drives rather than risk stimulating the domestic economy. Monetary and fiscal measures that might result in still larger government debt and higher taxes are held in reserve.

Japan's rapid economic advances since the war have now reached the stage where it has overtaken most of its competitors by many international comparisons. Even if one only takes the five years between 1977 and 1982 it leaves Japan with the highest average Gross Domestic Product growth rate, lowest inflation and, perhaps most topical of all, the lowest unemployment statistics. The process of modernization embarked on over a century ago is obviously over. Some commentators would go so far as to suggest that Japan, having completed its 'catch-up' period, is now out on its own with the ability to show the way to other industrial societies. Be that as it may, a nation that has rarely had even 2% of its work-force laid off between 1952 and 1982 deserves to be taken seriously by contemporary historians and social scientists.

Such achievements were not easily gained and industrialization in Japan, as elsewhere, has caused disruption and hardship. Fishing villages and coal-mining towns lost their *raison d'être*. Farmers sold out to developers. Families became separated as sons went to work on assembly lines in Aichi and Kanagawa prefectures. Yet hard graft was accepted, for there appeared to be few alternatives. Inadequate housing, cold factories and cramped trains had to be tolerated if conditions might improve later. They did, though Western images have often not yet caught up with the more recent boosts in living standards. Yet, it might be equally dangerous to swing to the other pole and imagine that the days of the work ethic are numbered. The competitive nature of Japanese society, re-inforced by the strictures of parents, make this improbable. Some relaxation has occurred and productivity in certain offices and public corporations, as opposed to industrial plants, may make officials despair of the future. But, if the manner in which Japan overcame the disruptions of the twin oil shocks is any guide, it would be premature to start writing Japan off.

A nation's identity, its pattern of thought and behaviour, changes more slowly than shifts in economic development or institutional reform. Japanese values have gradually altered over the four postwar decades but the stress on homogeneity at the national and societal level has persisted. To give a few examples. The Japanese prime minister could campaign in December 1983 in much the same manner as his predecessors have done. Knowledge that Japan has overtaken the West (by some yardsticks at least) is one useful rallying cry. Tanaka Kakuei, when running as premier, used to stress the strength of the yen against the dollar; Nakasone could hardly adopt that tactic but he would argue that 'before I became prime minister, Japan was pushed into a corner by others. Now the voice of Japan is being raised'. It is popular both to note Japan's economic progress and to argue that the nation is under threat from external forces. Nationalism is strong and the remainder of the world is seen, in that telling Japanese expression, to 'misunderstand' Japan.

Can one anticipate any diminution of this insularity? Japan's postwar advances have given many the opportunity to visit other nations, albeit in often very restricted fashion under the restraints of time and the propensity to travel in groups on Japanese carriers, but how much difference this may have made to popular perceptions is unclear. Group tours to Asian capitals may confirm existing prejudices and even strengthen a sense of racial superiority. Reactions to visits to the West can be more complex. Europe may be merely a cultural museum for some and the United States a warning of the consequences of encouraging a multi-ethnic society, yet others might return to question the economic priorities of Japan. More important than placing any hopes on tourism would be to encourage greater contact on the personal level. Educational exchange has hardly been attempted and will remain rare until the structure and attitudes of the academic and administrative staff of Japanese universities begin to alter. It is certainly the case that Japanese industry, under the pressure of the market, has been obliged to confront the world in a more determined manner than Japanese higher education has dreamt of. Yet a sense of difference and separateness is still at the heart of the Japanese identity. The nation, the family, the company, the school all recognize this and find it a far from deplorable state of affairs.

Social anthropologists and psychologists have cautioned the layman against using the term 'national character'. They, no doubt, have excellent professional reasons for warning us off, but historians are obliged to generalize if they want to be read at all and, so long as Japanese of quite disparate backgrounds and accomplishments continue to preface their remarks with reference to their shared identity, it will be tempting to assume that there are important cultural traits and, perhaps, certain personality types that predominate. It has already been suggested that one aspect of contemporary Japanese identity has been widespread involvement in groups that will make considerable demands on their members. A willingness to submerge one's own point of view in return for the protection and psychological security that membership will provide is common, as is also a wariness towards other potentially hostile groups. Political parties have their factions, university departments their opposing cliques and rival sections in trading companies may drink in different bars. All this may well contribute to the larger 'us' and 'them' pattern of much Japanese thinking towards non-Japanese.

What other patterns of behaviour are encouraged in Japanese society? Conformity, loyalty, deference, moderation in presenting one's own views and an acceptance of eventual decisions that are necessarily a compromise based on a rough consensus are all frequently claimed to be praiseworthy. No one seriously pretends that the realities of Japanese society correspond more than very approximately to these ideals, but children are taught in primary school and later to think of their classmates, and new employees in corporations will receive pep talks on co-operation that they will have at least to endure politely. Harmony is a goal, however, that has to be constantly worked towards and the need to stress it so often suggests to some that it might easily go missing. The tensions involved in working closely in small groups with individuals that one may dislike can be imagined and give rise to afterhours drinking bouts where one can speak one's mind more freely with less risk of offence being taken.

Solidarity is one side of the coin; the other is dissent. Any overseas traveller to Japan who has arrived at Narita Airport and been processed through what can only be described as a fortified encampment might quickly wonder if this was quite the harmonious nation he had heard and read so much about. Later inquiries on the planning delays for the

New Tokyo International Airport might re-inforce his doubts on the validity of claims for the efficiency and foresight of Japan's bureaucrats, particularly when he recalls the distance and time involved in reaching downtown Tokyo from an airport still with only one runway 18 years after its inception. Other examples can be cited to remind us that Japan too has its share of social problems. The streets of Japan's cities are safe, but this does not preclude a nasty underworld that supervises prostitution, gambling and protection rackets. Gangsters (*yakuza*) have ties also to the right-wing political fringe and have developed the clever habit of packing stockholders' meetings with their stouter members to prevent effective discussion of company business. The connivance of major corporations in this activity only perpetuates the fraud. Mutual trust is another Japanese attribute that can be challenged. It does not prevent the most detailed investigation of candidates' backgrounds before admittance to large enterprises or the habit of employing various dubious means to look into family registers and financial statements before the selection of marriage partners. Likewise, social and racial discrimination abounds. Burakumin and Koreans are at the bottom of the pile. Those of Korean ancestry, who have lived their entire lives in Japan, are ineligible for employment in public schools or the bureaucracy. Only recently have non-Japanese become eligible for professorships in national universities. But dissatisfaction with the status quo need not express itself in any political act. Few of those earning low wages attempt collectively to improve their position; most suffer in silence rather than risk jeopardizing an already precarious existence. Rocking the boat is a dangerous venture. Morale in Japanese enterprises is often far from at the fever pitch of accounts in the Western press, yet unionization is declining. The LDP may be less popular, but this has not particularly aided the opposition parties as the proportion of those claiming to have no party allegiance has increased and the turnout dropped. (It is below the British level but still far higher than the poor response to American presidential elections.)

A look at popular culture should tell us something about contemporary Japanese behaviour. At the broadest level it is frequently a combination of watching television, playing *pachinko* and drinking with work-mates before braving the long train journey home. But, of course, it is often more than merely TV for the sedentary and the occasional practice at the local golf range for the active, since whole areas of Japan's cities are set aside as entertainment quarters catering for most tastes and budgets.

The Japanese play hard. Within yards of the subway exit at any of the downtown intersections are scores of coffee shops, noodle restaurant chains, video-games parlours, bars, discos and, slightly away from the main thoroughfares, the Turkish bathhouses and 'love' hotels. The Western image of Tokyo after dark as peopled only by sybarites and the privileged few on expense accounts is fortunately erroneous. Unfettered by licensing laws and with limitless tolerance of noise, the areas are crowded from early evening until the last train leaves for the suburbs.

What conclusions can be drawn from this energy and din? Is it merely evidence of an affluent, mass society comparable in British terms to Soho–Blackpool–Piccadilly rolled into one? While there are similarities, such as the *lingua franca* of pop, the motorbike gangs and pub crawlers, there are also differences. Cramped and often distant Japanese housing discourages entertainment at home and explains the plethora of restaurants and the institution of the coffee shop that serves as a *de facto* office for salesmen, rendezvous and escape hole from the company round the corner. Housewives are rarely involved in their husbands' leisure activities. Company receptions and trips are for company employees only. Wives are expected to rule at home and usually have control of the purse for major family purchases and to dole out an allowance to their husbands. This division of labour leaves Japanese wives in a far stronger position than some might imagine from accounts in the Western press. There is undoubted discrimination against women at work – female graduates are often taken on as glorified tea girls – but once married the situation is more equitable. Husbands are permitted some freedom to roam afterhours yet have limited financial independence. The salaryman and his coterie can pay frequent visits to their favourite bar to relax from the tensions of the office or shop-floor, but at home they may be lesser breeds. Some fathers' contribution to family life is often little more than an occasional excursion with their children on either a Saturday afternoon or, more likely, a Sunday. The slowness with which Japanese enterprises have moved to eradicate Saturday morning working (only in 1983 did banks finally agree to close one Saturday in the month) inevitably, and quite deliberately, restricts the time and attention that a father can devote to his family. Take away Saturday morning attendance and the company loses a not inconsiderable hold over its employees. Smaller enterprises have been particularly reluctant to reduce their working week on both economic and psychological grounds.

If and when a family does go out together, its choice of destination is likely to be back into the downtown centres rather than outwards to the less-crowded regions. This willingness to return to the urban shopping and entertainment districts is dictated partly by the attractions of the cities and partly by the distances required for families in the Tokyo or Osaka conurbations to escape their environment. Willingly or not, most fathers accompanying their families on Sundays are likely to head for the branches of the major department stores that are a feature of Japanese life without any Western counterpart. Here the customer is king, since the Japanese consumer expects and generally receives both value for money and a great deal of service from attentive salespeople. Department stores take themselves seriously in other ways. Many of the exhibitions to be found in any Japanese city are sponsored and presented in the exhibition halls of stores. Japan would be culturally the poorer without these expensive and important displays. The size of the attendance figures on any Sunday at an exhibition, for example, of Impressionist paintings is evidence of the widespread Japanese interest in Western art and a clue perhaps also to the limits of its taste.

Japan is more a nation of spectators than participants in the realm of sport. Although most schoolboys are reared on baseball, few play this or any other game once they have left high school. The inadequacy of many urban sports facilities and the demands of the company over both work and leisure hours necessarily curtail opportunities for many. Golf remains the select preserve of the upper bourgeoisie and tennis has enjoyed something of a recent boom among the young. The sports centres that do exist are a telling commentary on Japanese social priorities, since they have frequently been constructed by urban companies as profit-making outlets rather than as community projects open to local residents. Far more males elect to visit the nearest race-course (hopelessly crowded on Sundays and without bookmakers), baseball park or pro-wrestling hall than take up jogging or locate a convenient municipal swimming pool. All this suggests why Japan's performance at international sporting events has been a bitter disappointment to the nation. Only in judo and volleyball has Japan won much distinction. It would dearly like to do better.

Many of these strictures over both the limits to leisure time and the lack of appropriate facilities may gradually lose their force. Contrary to popular perceptions, the average number of hours worked in Japan is lower than in Britain and only slightly higher than that of West Germany. The great differences which remain are over the scarcity of the five-day week and the reluctance of many employees to use up their entitlement to paid holidays. Only when this begins to change can one expect to see major shifts in the time available for leisure activities. The company continues to come first in the view of many Japanese. There may be some weakening of such attitudes among the young but too much ought not to be read into this phenomenon. The same salaryman who this year rushes to the ski slopes at the first available opportunity may shortly be putting in unpaid overtime as he comes up for promotion. Competition within the same year's entrants in a large enterprise is often fierce and personal priorities do switch.

For housewives there would appear to be a greater variety of leisure activities on offer as the traditional feminine arts of the tea ceremony and flower arrangement face competition from culture centres and keep-fit classes. Once mothers have got their youngest child off to primary school they may have time on their hands before their husbands return home late in the evening. Parent–Teacher Associations, cooking schools and, increasingly, a part-time job help to fill the void. Japanese companies remain, however, reluctant to re-employ women who had worked before their marriage and most housewives who can find work are obliged to accept low wages in manufacturing or service industries. The lack of government-sponsored day-care centres and the consequent rise of dubious, commercial 'baby hotels' is a further difficulty that faces young mothers who want to get back into the labour market. Greater use of female employees would require changes in management attitudes and alterations to Japan's labour laws that presently restrict the hours and conditions of employment. Japan's men continue to see their wives' place as the home. Traditional attitudes still persist and indeed are reinforced by pressure from parents and company managers. If the only job one can find is assumed to be little more than of a temporary nature before marriage then it is difficult to take work too seriously and thus the prejudices of the company are confirmed. Office ladies (OLs) may certainly be better educated than ever before but there is a limit to the ways in which one can receive company guests or answer the telephone. Not surprisingly, such women with considerable free time and money (many will still be living with their parents) form a valuable market for sports-goods manufacturers, department stores and travel agencies.

There are other sides to Japanese culture that also deserve mention. Western publishers can only look with envy at the size of the market for books and journals. A best-seller means something very much larger than a print run of 5,000 copies for a successful British novel. The cheapness of Japanese publications and the rarity still of public libraries contributes to the boosting of sales, as does the publicity associated with the nomination of titles for prestigious annual book awards. What do the Japanese read? The answer is a mixture of serious journals, glossy magazines, economic studies, 'How To . . . ' books on professional, social and sexual issues and an endless range of lurid comics (*manga*). Comics, not just the province of children, account for a quarter of the books and magazines published. Translations of Western literature and current affairs also proliferate. Works on American management techniques are seemingly assured of success, as are foreign descriptions of the current Japanese scene provided, perhaps understandably, they are sufficiently laudatory. Praise from Western sources is always welcome and can produce the slightly absurd situation of Japanese journalists reporting from Washington or New York the moment any front page story or magazine cover article appears, regardless of its content. Likewise, American television reportage from Tokyo or Kyoto to New York is instantly shown on Japanese screens, however trite or sensational it may be.

The two contemporary Japanese art forms best known to the West are the cinema and literature. Names such as Kurosawa Akira, Ozu Yasujiro and Mishima Yukio possess a sure niche, with retrospective surveys of postwar Japanese film being shown periodically in European and North American centres and translations of Mishima's works readily available in paperback. The Japanese cinema is deservedly accorded a great deal of respect. Kurosawa's films *Rashomon* and *Kagemusha*, separated in the making by 30 years, found popularity with two generations of audiences. Ozu's slow-moving accounts of the difficulties of Japanese family life have also had a considerable following abroad and there are some critics who have predicted a revival in the current fortunes of the Japanese cinema. Works, for example, by Oshima Nagisa have gained a certain notoriety in Europe, though the prudishness of Japan's censors has resulted in only stunted versions of his recent films being shown in his homeland. Most films made in Japan are less ambitious. The popular cinema continues to churn out the equivalent of pulp fiction with sentimental accounts of rural Japan, gangster movies, animated cartoons and vehicles for pop stars.

Mishima Yukio is undoubtedly the postwar Japanese writer best known to overseas readers. This has been through a combination of his literary merit and the flamboyance of his personality. His suicide in November 1970 was an international *cause célèbre*. It also greatly

increased interest in Mishima's earlier publications and the final
volume of *The Sea of Fertility* tetralogy that Mishima completed shortly
before his death. Critics were quick to praise the work, while deploring
the ultra-nationalism behind his foredoomed attempt to arouse Japan
from what he saw as its materialism and opportunism. Countless
theories were instantly minted to account for Mishima's action. The
Japanese premier told the press that Mishima must have been mad.
Others preferred to see the suicide as that of an ageing homosexual who
felt his best work was now behind him and whose obsession with death
was manifest.

One of Mishima's earliest literary sponsors was the writer Kawabata
Yasunari, who in 1968 was to become the first and, so far, only
Japanese author to gain the Nobel Prize for literature. Many have consistently maintained that either Tanizaki Junichiro or Mishima might
have been a more appropriate choice. Tanizaki, who had died in 1965,
had written during the Pacific war an immensely long and involved
family saga entitled *Sasame Yuki* (*The Makioka Sisters* was the English
title) that has a vibrance lacking in Kawabata's more melancholy fiction. A visually fine film version of *Sasame Yuki* was made in 1983 by
Ichikawa Kon, best known in the West for his film of the Tokyo
Olympics. It is a commentary on European interest in Japanese culture
that when Kawabata's Nobel Prize was announced none of his works
were then in print in English. Happily this situation has since been
rectified. His most popular works have been the early short story *The
Izu Dancer* and the novella *Snow Country*. Both have retained their
popularity through being made and remade in stage and film versions.
Younger generations, however, are likely to be impatient with the
themes and heroines of Kawabata and Tanizaki and turn instead to the
likes of Oe Kenzaburo and Abe Kobo for works of more contemporary
relevance.

Music is the one art form to have achieved widest acceptance in its
Western guise. The number and quality of orchestras in Japan testify
to music's popularity. Tokyo supports orchestras such as the New
Japan Philharmonic Orchestra, conducted by Ozawa Seiji, as well as
ballet and opera groups of a high standing. Concerts by celebrities of the
calibre of Horowitz or visiting companies with the *cachet* of the Royal
Ballet are certain to be sold out. Japan's musical exports to the West
include the Suzuki method for training young violinists, the Yamaha
piano and *karaoke*, an unfortunate invention whereby musical backing
encourages pub singers and infuriates neighbours. Theatre on the other

hand had a harder time of it. The language barrier immediately comes into force to restrict any potential audience. There is also competition from Japanese experimental drama and the classical *noh* and kabuki theatre forms which continue to have their bands of loyal followers.

Exponents in other fields where Japan has gained international recognition deserve to be at least mentioned. Modern architecture might be represented by Tange Kenzo, as witnessed by his overseas commissions, fashion by Yamamoto Kansai and Mori Hanae and Japanese food (and presentation) by its *sushi* masters. Japan has also a large number of talented photographers, illustrators and graphic designers whose careers have prospered in tandem with the growth of the Japanese advertising industry. It is perhaps appropriate that Japan's rapid postwar development had led to Japan boasting of the world's largest advertising agency. Despite the nation's artistic achievements and their influence on contemporary life, Japan in the last resort remains a business culture. Its values are those of the mass consumer society.

6

Japan in the 1980s: the Nakasone and Takeshita years

Nakasone Yasuhiro was prime minister of Japan for over five years. He held office for longer than any of his immediate predecessors and his term as premier from the autumn of 1982 to the autumn of 1987 has been exceeded only by Yoshida and his protégé Sato among his postwar peers. It proved in some ways an exhilarating era for those who had previously assumed that Japanese leaders were invariably faceless men who led equally grey cabinets. It is probably too early to reach any balanced judgment on Nakasone's achievements but a start may be made at a moment when commentators are noting how quickly he has been politely ignored by his successor and how easily Japanese politics has reverted to its former style.

Nakasone throughout his political career has found it difficult to disguise his ambitions or to inspire the trust and support required to scramble to the top of Japan's greasy pole. It was presumably for these reasons that he had to wait impatiently for his turn at the helm and why, once he had finally gained his chance, he made the most of his belated opportunity. Nakasone intended to alter portions of established domestic and foreign policy under the grandiose and suspect slogan of supervising the end of the postwar era. He wanted to change what he regarded as out-of-date practices and to create a more dynamic international role for a nation that he, as a former wartime Imperial Navy officer, regarded as unnecessarily deferential in international affairs. Recollections of the humiliation of Japan's defeat in the Pacific war and its enforced transformation during the occupation and after formed the basis for much that Nakasone attempted to do. He hoped to see Japan reevaluate the occupation reforms and shift to a more active foreign policy by acting in partnership with, rather than remaining subservient to, the United States. It was a large agenda and it was addressed to the Japanese public as much as to the inner circle of political, bureaucratic and business elites. The Nakasone years must now be assessed and his very considerable goals placed against his accomplishments. It is, of course, a mixed record, but Nakasone can be said to have gone some way to altering firmly established domestic behaviour and to take pride in having been the first Japanese premier in a generation to have cut an international figure. Nakasone's major interest was always foreign affairs, where he was eager to speak for Japan and to impress on overseas audiences in forcible terms the fact that Japan was no longer prepared to continue apologizing for past transgressions or willing to kowtow to others. Japan, in Nakasone's view at least, should start reminding international opinion that it had clearly articulated policies worthy of a decent hearing, from a nation that was becoming more than just a merchant state. The contrast between what one former American ambassador to Tokyo described a year before Nakasone became premier as only the gradual attainment of an independent foreign policy, despite the fact that 'world leaders still encourage Japan to take greater initiative in international matters rather than being a follower as it has been on most issues to date', and Nakasone's activism is decidedly marked.

Nakasone intended to educate both the Japanese people and their counterparts across the Pacific as to the realities of power. The premier wished to bestir Japan from its past timidity and explain to the United States that an approximately equal partnership with Washington would necessarily require a change in American attitudes. From the outset Nakasone intended to create waves in a most un-Japanese fashion. Less than a year after gaining office, through the assistance of Japan's then political kingmaker Tanaka Kakuei, the new premier was rightly being heralded as leading a new Japan that spoke up as a member of the West. This was all very different from the behaviour of his predecessor, who had visited Washington in May 1981 only to become embroiled in controversy over whether or not Japan and the United States shared an 'alliance' and whether it had been agreed that Tokyo would defend the shipping routes of the south China sea. Nakasone had long been portrayed in the Japanese media as a hawk intent on strengthening and revitalizing Japan's security forces, but he claimed that a greater contribution by Japan to the defence of home islands and the surrounding waters was necessary because of American dissatisfaction over what became popularly known as the 'free-rider' issue and, perhaps more importantly, because it was what Nakasone wanted for Japan. He had frequently insisted that Japan had to take defence issues more seriously and needed to strengthen its own security if its claims to being a major power were to be taken seriously by other states. While publicly acknowledging that Japan's three non-nuclear 'principles' were to be respected, the new premier spoke of his wish to 'continue to build up a quality defence force at the minimum level needed for the self-defence of Japan' and 'effectively maintain' the US–Japan security arrangements. What essentially changed during the Nakasone years in the realm of defence issues was not so much the pace of expansion (much had been at least promised earlier and partly realized) but consideration of where Japan stood and why it needed to proclaim its allegiance. Even the political debate over whether Japan should exceed the 1% of GNP limit on defence spending can be seen as evidence to confirm Nakasone's opinion on the unrealistic nature of much earlier commentary. The figure had become a shibboleth devoid of any military rationale, though seen by the left as a guard against a retreat to the 1930s, and deserved to be scrapped. For Japan to move fractionally over the previous defence limit and then for critics to proclaim that this was the beginning of the end for democratic government was patently absurd. Nakasone did succeed in asking more people to reconsider the basis for Japan's defence effort. In this exercise he was assisted by a gradual increase in public respect for the SDF's mission, which in turn was strongly influenced by a greater hostility towards the Soviet Union and concern that the United States was not the military force in the Asian-Pacific region that it had been before the loss of Saigon.

Nakasone's public endorsements of the strengths behind the US–Japan relationship were well received. By explaining that Japan had set its mind to greater cooperation in the defence field he was applauded by President Reagan and this led him to boast on his return to Tokyo of his personal ties to Reagan. The 'Ron–Yasu' tag gained Nakasone a great deal of publicity at home and abroad. Nakasone's assertiveness overseas was appreciated in Japan as confirmation that the postwar nation had come of age. The media attention on, for example, the annual advanced nations summits and the visits abroad of cabinet ministers is evidence of diminishing faith in either neo-isolationism or editorials on 'Japan's position as a pacifist nation'. The claim of the 1985 white paper on defence (reported in the press on 8 August) that Japan's military played as important a role as Japan's diplomatic and economic functionaries in safeguarding the nation's security was taken to reflect Nakasone's own views, as was the statement in the foreword to the 1987 white paper which spoke of the public as having begun 'to take realistic views on defence issues in light of the real domestic and foreign conditions'.

It remains, however, a process that has merely started. The Director General of the Defence Agency still had to caution in 1987 that 'the people do not as yet have adequate interest and understanding concerning some matters: why Japan must make defence efforts and why Japan must firmly maintain the US–Japan security arrangements and endeavour to ensure and strengthen its reliability'. Both Nakasone's aspirations and impatient US Congressional resolutions have had to reckon with considerable Japanese resistance from the public at large and their timid politicians. Yet over improvements to the Self-Defence Forces' equipment there has been some progress as new weaponry has been purchased from the United States, built under licence from American manufacturers or designed domestically. Orders for new generation fighter aircraft, anti-submarine patrol planes and fleet escorts suggest that support within Japanese society for a more substantial defence effort has emerged. The 1980s have seen regular annual increases in the national budget for defence (and foreign aid), and the Reagan administration went out of its way to applaud this commitment, while still pressing Tokyo to do more.

Appreciation of Japan's strengthening military role tempered US criticism over Japan's trading behaviour. President Reagan appears to have judged that Japan's attention to defence improvements during the Nakasone years more than balanced doubts on whether Japan was exerting a sufficiently constructive influence over international trade and finance. To know that Japan was committed to sharing in the defence of Western interests in the region was reckoned to be more valuable than penalizing Tokyo for refusing to import rice or silicon chips. Yet it has to be said that Nakasone's attempts to explain Japan's persistent trade imbalances convinced neither the American Congress nor his own people. Nakasone presided over an enormous expansion in Japan's balance of payments surplus and quite failed to persuade the Japanese public that it was ultimately in its own interests to begin to behave in a more 'international' manner. Nakasone's homely analogy that Japan had been for far too long the mahjong victor who would ultimately drive away the other players from the table found few converts. Instead Japanese industrialists and workers were no longer afraid to voice their belief that the rest of the world ought to stop complaining and roll up their sleeves instead of talking about Japan Inc. and non-tariff barriers.

Trade issues between Japan and the United States persisted throughout the 1980s, and it is safe to bet that they will continue to do so in the

next decade. Nakasone inherited the problem and passed the parcel on
to his successor. He began in 1982 with an economy that had already
demonstrated its resilience during the period between the two oil shocks
by having the highest international growth and productivity rates and
enviably low unemployment and inflation statistics. He bequeathed to
Mr Takeshita an even stronger economy that has yet again confounded
its critics by tackling and solving issues of currency change and industrial relocation. Nakasone's primary concern was the impact that the
piling up of trade surpluses continued to have on Japan–US relations
and, to a much lesser extent, it has to be said, with regard to disruptions
to Japan–EC and Japan–ASEAN ties. Nakasone was always more concerned with his links to Reagan and the American government, since the
US–Japan security relationship was never far from his mind. Nakasone's political style both aided and ultimately damaged his efforts over
trade diplomacy. The premier was quick to strike the dramatic gesture
and rush off to breakfast meetings with Congressional leaders, but the
substance behind his frequent statements on market openings and
import drives was slender. His much heralded promises rarely dented
(for American industries under siege, though less' rarely for the
American consumer) an alarming trade gap. Nakasone's television lecture to the Japanese public on the joys of buying foreign goods in the
spring of 1985 at a particularly tense moment in US–Japan trade negotiations elicited almost no support from the nation. The *Asahi
Shimbun*'s poll on the public's reaction announced that over 80% of the
Japanese public admitted that there were no foreign products that they
wished to purchase at present. What the electorate sought from Nakasone was rather a continuation of his diplomatic offensive; their expectation remained that all would yet come right.

Since Nakasone was proud of his personal connections to the Reagan
administration and welcomed the opportunity to personify his vision of
an assertive Japan, he must take his share of criticism for having failed
even to contain the economic and financial friction between Japan and
most of its trading partners. No Japanese politician, of course, could
have singlehandedly 'solved' the problem, but in some ways Nakasone
exacerbated the issues. His leadership rarely entailed more than the
making of bold promises, and he increasingly lacked the active cooperation of Japan's bureaucrats and politicians, without which little could
be done. In order to inject a degree of emergency into Japanese politics
Nakasone was ever willing to employ his own research groups,
academic contacts and reform committees to challenge the bureaucratic

establishment, but this ploy became increasingly ineffective as the
insiders fought back against these attempts to alter both existing
domestic and international policies.

Distinguished figures might cooperate with Nakasone in producing
reports on, for example, external economic issues, but the final hurdle
of how to implement the committee's recommendations frequently
remained to mock the premier. It was all very well for advisory groups
to lecture the government that it 'must not stop at short-term fixes but
must demonstrate clearly its determination to internationalize by
taking external economic measures from a medium and long-term
viewpoint', but this incessant call for internationalization often either
lacked content or came up against entrenched interest groups. The truth
was that for many American politicians and business leaders the very
existence of a massive trade deficit was seen as evidence that Japan's
markets were not open, and that only when the trade gap began to
shrink would these figures accept that Japan was now playing fair.
However, more recent popular American works have stressed that cultural differences make for difficulties that would take decades to correct
even if both sides were willing to cooperate. Politicians, of course,
operate everywhere under a very restricted time scale and are not
answerable to a transpacific constituency. Since Japan posted a record
94 billion dollar surplus in 1986, as opposed to 24 billion in fiscal 1983,
the criticism was predictable.

The best that Nakasone could produce in the way of stemming parts
of the overseas onslaught was, appropriately enough given the manner
in which he operated, a series of recommendations by a personal advisory group. The Maekawa report of 1986 will long remain the feather in
Nakasone's economic cap, for it at least began the serious business of
restructuring the Japanese economy and publicized the extent of what
critics had taken to describing as the 'Japan problem'. The Maekawa
report, named after its author, who had previously been governor of the
Bank of Japan, urged upon the nation the need to grow under its own
steam rather than depend on exports to the United States and elsewhere.
Evidence from Japanese governmental sources suggest that in 1986 and
1987 the economy did precisely as ordered by showing impressive leaps
in domestic demand and negative growth in the case of exports. All this
contrasts significantly with the early Nakasone years, when it was a rise
in exports that enabled real growth to spurt ahead, but courage would
be required by industrialists, politicians, and economic bureaucrats if
Maekawa's prescriptions were to be sustained on into the 1990s. Public

attention on what may be a shift in Japan's trading behaviour should not leave one imagining that trade issues have been wiped off the agenda. The strengths of Japan's manufacturing industries remain as impressive as ever. Two items of news announced on the same morning in January 1986 demonstrate that much is still well with its enterprises: NEC reported that it had replaced Texas Instruments as the world's top semiconductor company in terms of estimated sales, and Toyota said that it had produced its 50th million car, with its president warning that this should not be an excuse for relaxation as the next target was to overtake General Motors. Rival industrialists in the West will still campaign to restrict Japanese exports, and it appears probable that new sectors will have to face the competition that has been so damaging for others during the past generation. Beyond trade friction will be more trade friction.

The very considerable appreciation of the yen (*endaka*) against the dollar by the late 1980s has damaged some Japanese industries for good, particularly those less reliant on high value added product. Yet even though labour-intense, cheaper manufacturings have increasingly been processed offshore in Japanese-owned factories in Taiwan, Hong Kong and Singapore, it would be erroneous to imagine that there has been a complete 'hollowing out' of less advanced, less skilled assembly work. Cutlery, simple electronic goods and some textiles, however, will certainly decline under the *endaka* shifts but, brutal though it may appear, such dualistic firms were destined to go under as the newer developing nations of the Pacific rim flex their muscle and follow in Japan's path to modernization.

Yet of perhaps even greater long-term consequence is Japan's rapid emergence as a dominant global financial power. If the trade surplus more than trebled during the Nakasone premiership so too did Japan's external assets. By 1988 the top seven banks in the world ranking and indeed eighteen of the first thirty were based in Tokyo or Osaka. This rise has been so rapid and its impact potentially so vast that the West has yet to be fully aware of what is occurring in this formidable and seemingly ineluctable challenge to the New York and London financial markets.

Estimates of the future strengths of Japan's financial sector obviously vary, but continued improvement at least well into the 1990s seems probable. One recent study has suggested that Japan's international capital surplus will have doubled by 1995 and it is possible that any improvement of this magnitude will be accompanied by international confrontations comparable to those that have long occurred in the trading sector. The so-called 'second-wave' may prove as difficult to contain for Japan's politicians and bureaucrats as the present trade friction. Yet at the moment there is no doubting the necessity for the West of encouraging Japan to act as an overseas investor. Japanese banks and financial institutions regularly bid for sizeable chunks of the monthly offerings of US Treasury bonds and it is Japanese institutions who have underwritten a third of the bank funding behing the launching of the Anglo-French Eurotunnel project. Explanations as to why Japan has quite suddenly become such an important player (perhaps *the* international financial figure) must start with the very high savings rates of Japanese families. Certainly the trend for the last decade has been downward but the flood of money entrusted to Japanese banks, post offices, insurance companies and security houses is now too large for Japan's domestic institutions to absorb, and consequently portions of it have been used as capital exports. The evidence of Japan's presence abroad can be seen in the City of London, where there are over seventy Japanese security firms and nearly thirty banks. It needs to be noted that Japanese banks and security firms have done much better abroad than their American and European competitors in Japan, although the explanations for this discrepancy are not entirely clear. Certainly some characteristics of Japanese business assist in keeping the foreign bank at a disadvantage (and hence more likely to deal with some of the riskier corporations) by stressing the long-term nature of client relationships, lower interest rate charges and solicitous after-sales services. Financial commentators doubt whether all of the large number of non-Japanese institutions in Tokyo are yet breaking even; as with the European dreams of the fabled nineteenth-century China market, the reality can be chastening.

For the Japanese public, however, it was not foreign affairs or financial expansion that was at the centre of their interest in Nakasone's behaviour. The policy area where Nakasone made his largest impact for the salary worker and his family was over domestic reform. This field was yet another where the premier attempted a great deal and had at the end of the day to be satisfied with rather less than he had aspired to. Nakasone took office against a need to reduce the Japanese government's deficit and to prepare for a future where demands on the welfare state (parts of it of very recent origin) were certain to rise as medical costs increased with an aging society. The premier adopted the theme of administrative reform as the hallmark of his cabinets, and was able to gain some cost savings by privatizing former government monopolies (telephones and tobacco) and by hiving off Japan National Railways into regional entities. Many of these schemes were pushed through only in the teeth of considerable resistance, and suggest that Nakasone could enforce structural reform when he put his mind to it. Unfortunately for Nakasone, his failure to persuade his own party of the merits of an overhaul of the taxation system, which had remained virtually intact since its inception during the occupation era, led to his downfall in 1987. The entire subject of tax reform has long been a graveyard for Japanese premiers, and Nakasone was neither the first nor probably the last to meet with electoral defeat on the issue. The need to alter the strong direct taxation element behind Japanese governmental revenues has long been popular with white-collar workers, since too many favoured groups have been granted remarkably generous concessions or blatant opportunities for tax evasion in the past. The problem has invariably been the power of such elements (particularly farmers, small businessmen and doctors) to remind the LDP of why their special treatment should be continued. Nakasone failed for two reasons. First it was widely felt that his tax programme went against an election pledge made before his sweeping victory in the July 1986 campaign, and secondly, many feared that the initial sales tax (set at 5%) could be easily enlarged as and when future governments judged fit.

Unlike numbers of his countrymen Nakasone is an unashamed nationalist. This at times got him (deservedly) into hot water. He could make disparaging remarks about minorities within Japan and the United States, while all too easily praising the racial composition and social unity of the Japanese. It would have been better if Nakasone had kept his mouth shut, but such opinions are widespread within Japanese society and, while not to be defended, his comments are commonplace. What the prime minister tried to do was to encourage his nation to review the past and to take a more adventurous stance in world affairs. His belief that Japan could hardly be regarded as a sovereign state unless its government and people began to adopt a greater role in their own defence is one that he had long promoted, and his argument that Japan's economic power required appropriate support for the international trading system ought to have been obvious, if only in terms of national self-interest. It is, however, a measure of the retreat and caution of the postwar decades that Nakasone's remarks should have been seen as controversial in pleading for greater realism in military and foreign policies. If Japan was not prepared to stand up and cooperate with its allies it risked, to adopt the warning of Nakasone's predecessor, becoming once again 'an orphan in the world'.

Nakasone's years in office witnessed a brave attempt to encourage change in Japanese domestic and overseas behaviour. The difficulty for the premier was the clear lack of agreement, however, within Japanese society as to the direction that Japan ought to take and the sometimes timid response of his fellow politicians to his calls for fresh thinking. Nakasone's assertiveness and his association with nationalistic symbols of prewar and wartime Japan also made the going harder for him. Indeed, he may have been a prime minister whose appeal would have been more suited to the next decade when Japan would have better digested its recent economic, financial and political advancement. Nakasone held that a degree of short-circuiting of the existing political and bureaucratic alignments was necessary to galvanize the public, but the electorate was rarely prepared for this approach, and preferred to let the professionals solve the problems in the conventional way. The zeal of Nakasone and the constant foreign pressure only stiffened the resistance of some and left his ambitions far from fulfilled. He was respected for speaking up for Japan, but rejected when he demanded of his nation that radical rethinking was the order of the day. What Nakasone did best was to make Japanese politics more stimulating. He began the process of education and persuasion whereby the gulf between economic strength and international caution might be later narrowed. Nakasone's reputation may yet revive once the latent forces he represents are eventually given their head.

Nakasone's long tenure ended when he personally selected Takeshita Noboru to be his successor in October 1987. The appointment was made by Nakasone in his capacity as president of the LPD, since the rival candidates for his post were prepared to accept this unprecedented selection procedure in order to avoid the very considerable financial and psychological costs of conducting an elaborate party election campaign. It was then widely claimed that the new leader would be under some personal obligation to Nakasone for his appointment and that the older figure would insist on a behind-the-scenes role in policy making. It did not work out quite like that. Takeshita quickly became his own man and was able to lead a party that has rarely been as friction- and faction-free.

Mr Takeshita's first year in office was neither particularly exciting nor successful. His accomplishments, besides firmly stamping his power on the party and distancing himself from his predecessor, were slim. The new leader made a fair start in the international field and was able to win parliamentary approval for a tax reform bill that he had inherited in outline from Nakasone, but the pace was deliberately slow and the agenda unclear. There was little of the sparkle of the Nakasone years, and a general sense that politics could be reduced to merely continuing with existing economic policies and containing overseas comlaints in the areas of trade and finance without treading on too many domestic toes. Criticism of Takeshita centred on his lack of vision and his confidence that problems were best aired and solved in private away from the floor of the Diet and the intrusions of the media. Until the first months of 1989, however, it had appeared probable that Takeshita's performance would be rewarded with a second two-year term as his party's leader. If there had been little to write home about, it had to be said in Takeshita's defence that the economy had continued to boom and there were fewer foreign complaints over Japan's international behaviour. Takeshita's Japan appeared to be taking note of American requests in both the security and economic spheres. The earlier stress on exporting was gradually being replaced by stronger domestic demand and consumer spending, while in budgetary terms at least the prime minister could point out to Washington that his nation was endeavouring to rearm in depth and offering substantially more foreign aid to developing states. The change of American president and the appointment of Michael Armacost as the successor to Ambassador Mansfield may put more flesh on the current diplomatic rhetoric of 'burden sharing' between the two Pacific allies. The difficulties, however, of persuading the Japanese public to do more, and the adjustment that would be required of the United States if co-partnership became a reality, should not be ignored. Much depends on how the prime minister and his advisers respond and the attention given from the centre to the question of Japan's global role.

Yet gradually Takeshita found himself embroiled in a major financial scandal and by the spring was having to fight for his political life. As with his battle to alter Japan's taxation system, the premier responded by adopting his familiar behind-the-scenes tactics, and prevaricated when challenged in the Diet to tackle the problem in a direct, public manner. The result has been that the details continued to dribble out piecemeal and the press sensed blood. The government's expectations that the scandal involving the wholesale attempt by an ambitious information and publishing company, Recruit, to offer inducements in the form of pre-flotation stock purchases to a large number of politicians, businessmen, bureaucrats, academics and journalists would quietly fade away have been dashed. The revelations and indictments by a particularly vigorous Tokyo district prosecutor have produced Japan's most serious postwar political scandal. It remains to be seen how Takeshita can overcome his rather feeble promises to introduce substantial political reforms, after having already been obliged to accept the resignation of senior members of his cabinet and failing to accurately gauge the changing public reaction to insider trading and the complacency of the LDP to the whole affair.

The Recruit scandal would not disappear even during the weeks of the long anticipated death and funeral of Emperor Showa. The Emperor's death can not be said to have prompted any particularly profound debate on the sixty-two years of his reign. While he was terminally ill with cancer (a fact generally known but left vague in keeping with Japanese medical tradition) portions of the nation went through at least the outward motions of 'restraint' out of respect for the Imperial family, but it was hard to discern any great introspection after his death in January 1989. Discussion on his wartime role and the nature of the throne in contemporary Japan was muted. Conservative voices in the media spoke of his 'gentle' personality and his 'unfathomly great' achievements, while the JCP attacked such respectful remarks as 'a distortion of history' and thought it absurd to regard Japan's postwar prosperity as being linked to his behaviour. Most of the prewar and wartime generations appeared sympathetic towards the person of the Emperor and subscribed to the view that he had possessed little or no authority to challenge decisions made elsewhere in his name. The youth of Japan only 'discovered' their Emperor when he was ill and many remained apathetic when encouraged to consider the nature of Japanese imperialism. Some voices in Europe and Asia, however, were stridently critical and refused to forgive or forget the Pacific, Chinese and southeast Asian campaigns. The contrast between the Japanese and German attitudes towards the fascist era was only underlined when Takeshita said that 'it should be judged by historians whether or not Japanese wartime acts were invasion' and further compounded the problem by adding that it was 'hard' to label Hitler's behaviour in the Second World War in Europe as aggression.

Japan in 1989 did not employ the circumstances of the death and funeral of the late Emperor to confront the past. The Japanese nation had still to adequately come to terms with its earlier imperialism. Until this is attempted there will be clear restraints on any genuine global political role because of continuing domestic hesitancy and Asian suspicions. Encouragement by the United States for Japan to shed its self-imposed restraint has yet to carry the day in areas beyond the economic and financial fields. The unprecedented number of foreign dignitaries who flew to Tokyo for the funeral ceremonies of Emperor Showa returned home having recognized Japan's extraordinary economic successes but with little assurance that its foreign policies would alter in the medium term.

Much the same lack of vision is apparent in domestic affairs. The environmental problems persist, with the consequences of low-density housing and unplanned development all too visible. The result remains an unlovely urban sprawl. Cabbage patches sit amidst shopping centres and love hotels and golf driving ranges cluster against jerry-built apartments. The political clout of highly subsidized weekend farmers, collecting minuscule crops engulfed by factories and schools, permits them to hold out against the commuter tide until real estate speculators can entice them to sell up. Only greater governmental controls would alter this dismal picture, and until that improbable day the supposedly affluent salary worker has little prospect of purchasing a small family house on even the very edge of Tokyo. Although the Japanese are increasingly richer in pocket and are beginning to enjoy longer holidays, as some corporations follow the example of banks and the stock markets and close for the long weekend, little appears to change in their surroundings. The consumer too gets a raw deal at home, though quickly appreciating the buying power of the yen when abroad. Imported goods remain overpriced. The distribution system is still convoluted. Special interest groups continue to monopolize the seats of power in the LDP and the bureaucracy. Japan is still a first-class economic power hobbled by a third-rate political structure.

Postscript

Eventually in the wake of the Recruit scandal Prime Minister Takeshita was obliged to resign. He was succeeded after an extended search for a 'clean' figure by Uno Sousuke in June 1989. The prospects for the LDP were bleak. The public remained unimpressed with the professions of shame and guilt by the conservatives and a general disillusionment with government was widespread. Uno had the difficult task of attempting to clean out the stables without upsetting his party. He spoke up against political corruption but could hardly be expected to dismantle his party in the process. Factions have not been dissolved and fundraising continues unabated. Fortunately for the LDP the disunity of the opposition camp under Ms Doi Takako and doubts over its competence to lead a coalition cabinet may yet spare the conservatives from the defeat that they deserve. Forecasts of 4 to 5% economic growth for the medium-term future and the need to resist overseas trading pressures could still prove a winning hand for a party that has become stiff at the joints. However, Mr Uno was himself forced to resign in late July to take responsibility for his party's humiliating defeat in the Upper House elections caused by anger over his personal life and the unpopularity of the new sales tax. Frantic searches then began to unearth a successor who might hold the party together and restore some credibility to what was increasingly turning into a demoralized team. All was not yet lost, but the conservatives were suddenly in the deepest of trouble.

7

The future: Japan today and tomorrow

The general election held in December 1983 was a setback for the LDP and an even more serious blow to the personal position of Prime Minister Nakasone. The results left the LDP approximately where it had been before the June 1980 double election had boosted the party's strength. What was different this time was the rapid action of the party managers to repair the damage and prevent a long drawn-out public feud over responsibility for the loss of 36 seats. Confusion was prevented by three means. First a small number of independents were invited to join the ranks of the LDP in order to demonstrate that the party had once again an absolute majority in the Diet. Then, to the surprise of many within and without the party, it was announced that a coalition had been formed with the breakaway New Liberal Club by which the NLC would support the government in return for a cabinet appointment and influence over the direction of forthcoming legislation. Lastly, the selection of personnel to head the three senior LDP posts and the remaining cabinet seats was seen to reflect more equitably the factional strengths of rival LDP groups. It was widely interpreted as an admission by Nakasone that the days of earlier dominance by the Tanaka faction might be coming to an end. Within one week of the election a new government had been formed and sworn into office. The party had managed to avoid a repetition of the poisonous in-fighting that had continued so publicly from the October 1979 election until the May 1980 dissolution. Faced with a threat to its hold on power, the LDP had quickly pulled itself together and demonstrated once again that it could still govern. The stockmarket was relieved. The public went back to preparing for the new year celebrations. The crisis, at least for the moment, was over.

An examination of the 1983 election results suggests that it would be premature to assume that the LDP is likely to forfeit office in the 1980s. Several political scientists who made predictions a decade ago on probable coalition partnerships based on the LDP's decline would rather forget their earlier hypotheses. (The present partner in the LDP coalition only came into existence in 1976 and there are rumours aplenty that the NLC may well have joined with the conservatives in order eventually to form a merger.) What do the voting figures tell us of Japan's present mood and the future possibilities? First the size of the LDP's popular vote decreased less than 2%, while the JSP's share increased by an insignificant fraction. What was of importance was less the relative stability of votes cast for all the parties than the changes in the number of seats won. This came about for several reasons. The LDP, as has often happened in the past, was felt to have put up too many candidates and therefore lost seats that it ought otherwise to have captured. This was widely attributed to the eagerness of the Tanaka faction to demonstrate its strength and emphasize that the verdict of the Tokyo district court was not necessarily endorsed by the electorate. Tanaka's group failed to increase its size but came out of the election far better than its rivals. Tanaka himself won a resounding victory in his own Niigata constituency, thanks in part to intervention by a well-known novelist who drew votes away from the left-wing candidates. Gratitude, however, for Tanaka's undoubted efforts to haul his region out from the backwaters of Japan by the construction of a major series of public-works programmes played a larger role in his victory. The seemingly disgraced politician received 220,000 votes, the largest number cast for any one candidate across the nation.

Faulty organization by the LDP, coupled with an unwillingness by the prime minister to discuss the question of political ethics and doubts over the direction of his foreign policies, hurt the party. The lowest voting turnout in any postwar election (67.94%) was attributed to a decision by wavering LDP supporters to abstain. This was in sharp contrast with the ability of the Komeito to garner nearly all its potential vote. Komeito won 59 seats – as in the LDP's case, this was almost exactly the same total it possessed in 1979 before the 1980 election had badly dented the party's strength – to trounce the JCP and DSP for the title of second largest opposition party. It now has a 20-seat lead over the DSP and 32 seats more than the JCP.

The election campaign saw some attempts at co-operation by the opposition groups, though it was immediately apparent once the results were announced that there was no prospect of an anti-LDP coalition. The suggestion floated by the recently appointed JSP chairman Ishibashi Masashi that a joint opposition candidate be sponsored to oppose Nakasone when the Diet voted on its choice of premier was rejected by the centralist parties. Similarly the decision by the NLC to abandon its criticisms of the LDP and join the government camp was greeted with charges of betrayal by the remaining opposition parties. Numerous rank and file members of the NLC felt unease at the speed with which their party had switched sides. The leadership justified its actions by claiming that it could better achieve its goals of cleaning up politics and promoting educational and administrative reforms by linking its fortunes to the LDP.

Where did all this manoeuvring leave the prime minister? His political touch was best seen after the general election when he moved fast to quell dissatisfaction, split the opposition and organize his second cabinet. Where Nakasone had been less sure had been in the timing and conduct of the campaign. His record since gaining the post he had long coveted was not a particularly easy one to defend. He had tended to move Japan perhaps further and faster than public opinion thought wise in a pro-American direction. He had also done little to stimulate the economy. He had almost certainly been too cautious over avoiding criticism of the political influence of Tanaka within LDP councils. The result was interpreted as a personal rebuff for the premier, who had in addition to stomach the disappointment of coming second in his Gumma constituency to his old rival Fukuda Takeo. The reshuffling of posts as a consequence of the December election was seen by political commentators to imply a determination by Nakasone to gain re-election as LDP president in the autumn of 1984. The new secretary general of the party is a staunch Nakasone aide and efforts have been made to restrict the promotion of younger, rival candidates who might be able to show their mettle in government. What appears probable is that loss of LDP seats will require greater consideration by the party of opposition points of view – even with the *de facto* NLC coalition it will not be able to gain the chairmanship of all parliamentary committees – and a return to a quieter foreign policy. The next general election may tell us more about whether the LDP can continue to secure power on its own terms.

Financial scandals are endemic to Japanese politics. The necessity of tapping vast financial resources to compete for office creates repeated stories of kickbacks, dubious loans, and pressure on both companies and labour organizations to support certain candidates. The largest scandals have, not surprisingly, involved parties in power at the time. The Showa Denko affair had the most serious results. It brought to an end an already shaky period of coalition rule led by premier Ashida in 1948 and ended the hopes of the left being regarded as the natural party of government. In the light of later scandals it ought to be noted that the final verdict on those accused of taking bribes from the Showa Denko company was not delivered until 1962. The shipbuilding scandal of 1954 and 'black mist' stories of the 1960s next discredited but hardly undermined the continuation of LDP rule. More important though for the future of the party was the long-drawn-out Lockheed scandal that surfaced in 1976 and remains in 1984 a convenient symbol of the close links between the ruling party and big business.

It is a complex story that the courts have had to unravel. The public's main interest in the case has been to follow the role of former prime minister Tanaka, who was charged with bribery and sentenced to four years in prison by the Tokyo District Court in October 1983. His lawyers immediately appealed to the Tokyo High Court and it is widely believed that a further adverse ruling there would almost certainly be followed by appeal to the Supreme Court. The end of the drama is clearly not yet in sight. The central legal issue has been whether Tanaka, in his capacity as premier, had the power to persuade All Nippon Airways to purchase Lockheed TriStar aeroplanes by giving directions for orders of new generation aircraft to the transport minister at a time of intense rivalry between American companies and their respective Japanese selling agents. The prosecution maintained that Tanaka had used his influence and had been rewarded with ¥500 million for his pains. Tanaka has consistently denied the charges.

The ramifications of the Lockheed scandal have been considerable. In terms of adverse publicity for the LDP the impact would seem readily apparent, yet this has not prevented Tanaka from being re-elected and several other politicians who were found guilty of accepting bribes have also been returned to the Diet. It is always much easier to criticize when those held responsible for illegalities do not represent your district, where they may well have built up strong personal ties and worked to persuade the central government to improve local transportation links and educational facilities. Part of the Japanese electorate is highly conscious of the benefits to be gained by having representatives with bureaucratic backgrounds in the Diet likely to be of assistance in the fight for governmental funds. The politics of the pork barrel are serious matters for localities that lack good communications or adequate hospitals. LDP politicians from the more powerful factions are quick to exploit such anxieties. The fact that Kyoto has invariably ranked last in prefectural lists for infrastructural investment per head is evidence of central governmental neglect when the area had long preferred reformist politicians.

Yet the LDP's losses in the December 1983 election were probably at least partly attributable to the government's weak stance over political ethics. The clear influence of Tanaka on the first Nakasone cabinet made the voicing of such opinions difficult, but the issue persisted since few LDP figures were prepared to face it openly. The public expected at least a formal recognition of the cabinet's endeavour to change its behaviour. After the election had put the LDP's majority in jeopardy some belated attempts were made to commence reform. How much influence these changes may have on the conduct of future Japanese politics is doubtful. The need for massive financial donations appears ineradicable for the present. At least it might be claimed that the Lockheed scandal brought the subject out into the open and that this is highly desirable. Recent efforts by Elizabeth Drew in the *New Yorker* to draw attention to the many problems that face campaign funding in the United States and the widespread feeling in Britain that local government is not all it ought to be are reminders that the issue of corruption is not Japan's alone.

The issue of administrative reform is one that is unlikely to go away in the 1980s. Public hopes that drastic measures might be taken to curtail the increase in what many regard as unnecessary or excessive governmental expenditure have been high. They have also been partly disappointed with the efforts so far to stem the growing size of the budget deficit. The best that the supporters of administrative reform can point to has been the creation of a ceiling on present government expenditure. The crisis has its origins in the measures of the LDP in the early 1970s to increase simultaneously pension and welfare benefits and encourage regional development without raising adequate revenue to match these new outlays. Japan by the mid 1980s had seen its portion of GNP devoted to governmental expenditure rise from approximately 20% in 1970 to around 35% by 1984. Fears were voiced that the percentage might, if not quickly checked, begin to approach that of other advanced industrial nations. Some held this to be dangerous in that excessive coddling of industry and easy access to what was fast becoming a welfare state might create a Japan unable to maintain an adequate growth rate for an ageing population. A more partisan objection to possible increases in taxation levels was that this inevitably hurt the LDP by giving the opposition parties a free target.

The commission on administrative reform, headed by Doko Toshio, found it difficult to produce concrete proposals that could offer immediate results. The press complained that instead of governmental reconstruction without tax increases the process had been reversed. Expectations may have been too high but the public could hardly fail to note the timidity of the commission's recommendations. How is the government to placate the pressure groups that assail it on all sides, while recognizing that there remains a strong groundswell in favour of reducing expenditure? The decisions taken in the compilation of the national budget provide the best answer. A few items have been spared the knife (aid and defence in particular), but the 1983 budget has been called the most austere since 1955 with only a minimal increase over the previous year. This was necessary since government expenditure had dipped slightly from 1982 and the LDP was reluctant to talk of tax increases in an election year. By 1984 the cabinet was left with even fewer alternatives. In fact, late in 1983, it had given a small income tax cut as a present to the electorate (under pressure from the opposition), and to claw back funds it seemed certain to have to impose future indirect tax increases and authorize the flotation of still larger numbers of governmental bonds. The budget deficit continues to grow. It was calculated to have reached 6% of Japan's GNP by 1983 (approximately the same as in the United States) and economists have predicted further increases in the medium term. Some have argued that the propensity of the Japanese people to save – unlike the situation in the United States – makes the position containable, since government deficits can easily be funded in this manner. While this is true, it remains the case that additional bond-financing will impair the recovery of the economy and raise domestic interest rates.

The latest proposal from the administrative reform advisers in December 1983 has been to press for cuts in government subsidies and to hold down the pay of local government officials (a move certain to be popular with most citizens), while relying on private industry to provide improvement in the general economic condition. The government responded by announcing plans to increase corporation tax and to add new indirect taxes. Neither set of measures, however, would begin to tackle the existing government deficit, let alone make any reduction in what appears to be a permanent albatross that successive governments have come no nearer to removing. The difficulties of restraining public spending are in no way unique to Japan, but its public fears that unless a more determined strategy is employed shortly the problem could get out of hand. Identification of the issue is easy; finding a solution will present a daunting challenge to any politician prepared to take on the task in earnest.

Economic advancement has led to a reluctant and gradual re-evaluation of Japan's relations with the rest of the world. The issue of redesigning parts of Japan's foreign policy has been a slow starter. Gaining a bureaucratic or political consensus for change will be difficult, though this no doubt is commonly the case in any system of government which can easily pit section against section and political faction against faction. There has been much discussion in journals and newspapers on the type of foreign policy most desirable for Japan, but any analysis has to reckon with global events that either have not been or cannot always be foreseen. Japan, for example, has yet to complete the construction of its Iranian petrochemical project which was begun under the Shah. Its entire progress has been marred by setbacks as Japan reacted to the Iranian revolution and then the Iran–Iraq war. Mitsui, in what was its largest ever overseas investment, has been encouraged by the Japanese government to persevere, in the hope that its commitment will bring later returns to Japanese trading companies and goodwill for the Japanese government. Yet prestige projects of this magnitude are hostages to fortune and can be gambles that come badly unstuck.

It is the risk of closely linking economic and foreign diplomacies that Japan has generally attempted to avoid since the war. Its perceptions remain those of a trading nation wishing to shun the errors of the 1930s and 1940s. The trend since 1952 has been seen by some historians as a repeat of Japan's efforts in both the economic and political fields in the 1920s to adhere to what was then known as the Anglo-American school of diplomacy, with its stress on co-operative economic and commercial relationships. The popular view is that Japan should remain a merchant (*chonin*) rather than a warrior (*bushi*) state. The difficulty of the former is the probability of friction between trying to gain economic ends and having to accept political setbacks or even something that the public might regard as nearer to a humiliation. The wish to secure an adequate supply of oil from the Middle East has led to serious disagreements with the United States and shown up the dilemmas that Japan faces by trying to be friends with all sides. The apologies, for example, that the Japanese government felt obliged to give to the United States in 1979 for the actions of certain Japanese companies in disregarding the sanctions which Washington had persuaded its allies to adhere to after the seizure of the US embassy in Tehran were decidedly unpopular in Tokyo.

The securing of raw materials and natural resources is certain to remain at the centre of Japanese foreign policy. Its aid and cultural activities will continue to be geared to making new friends and strengthening existing relationships within the framework of resource diplomacy. For much of its necessary food imports, wheat and soya beans in particular, this ought not to present any great difficulty to future Japanese governments. It knows that it can almost certainly rely on the United States, Canada and Australia for these essential imports. (Some residue of doubt still lingers, however, as a consequence of the Nixon administration's decision in 1973 to curtail temporarily soya bean exports to Japan.) For oil, the position, as we have suggested, is likely to present more cause for anxiety, though hardly alarm, as the power of OPEC wanes and the price of oil stabilizes. Japan, of course, is vulnerable in the light of the extent of its dependence on overseas suppliers, but its financial muscle gives it opportunities that others hardly possess to buy its way out of tight corners. Such fears, too, go some way to explaining the government's determination to protect its agricultural interests. So long as a decent portion of its food is grown domestically, the system of subsidies and support prices will persist and the consumer will lose again to the Ministry of Agriculture.

The United States is clearly the nation with whom Japan will continue to associate most closely and on whom Japan will remain dependent for military assistance. It would seem probable that the United States will likewise continue to press unsuccessfully for an improved Japanese defence commitment and have to accept a rather disappointing response from a wary Japan. The present American ambassador to Japan (and doubtless his successors) will be obliged to make private and public statements encouraging not so much the expansion of the Japanese military as the maintenance by the government of the day of existing defence plans. Unless the global balance of power were to change dramatically, it is difficult to imagine that any Japanese government would be willing to accept the domestic political risks involved in expanding the SDF, knowing too that its neighbours might interpret such action as provocation. Japan, as we saw earlier in regard to its policies towards China and the Middle East, is quite capable of taking an independent course in foreign policy when it judges this essential, but will think twice before acting in disregard of American advice. It may be that the strengthening of the United States' Asian military posture through higher defence expenditure by the Reagan administration has gone some way to confounding those Japanese critics who have seen the debacle of Vietnam and self-doubts at home as evidence of an American loss of confidence and likely retreat from the region to better concentrate on the correction of its own domestic affairs.

The nature of Japan's future economic diplomacy with the United States and western Europe can be estimated with greater assurance. The growth of the Japanese economy more or less guarantees that its trading partners will find fault with Japan. The Japanese public will think this largely sour grapes and Western politicians will find it tempting to believe that the increase in Japan's share of international trade is the result of Japanese opportunism. The EC will continue to issue reports saying that the Japanese market is closed and the United States bureaucracy will produce similar findings, while others on transnational committees (often ex-diplomats and academics) will point to different conclusions. Each tends to preach to its own converts. The exercise will probably change few minds. In the meantime Japan will have felt obliged to agree to still more trading pacts that stipulate its market share of specific exports to designated countries. The slogan of free trade will be replaced by that of fair trade. The Japanese government, assuming that it can persuade its industrialists of the necessity of such practices, will see the arrangements as the only likely alternative to protectionism. It faces the danger, however, that once consent has been given to apparently temporary trading arrangements, they will persist. Such is possible, for example, in the important case of car restrictions to the United States. This was originally intended to be of a limited duration but may be extended indefinitely. Detroit, at least, can be relied on to attempt such a measure. Any Japanese response to such moves by the United States would be very carefully monitored by western European industrialists.

The boot may also be on the other foot in the future. We can expect to see more headlines along the lines of that recently in the *Oriental Economist* entitled 'New Twist in Trade Friction: Japan the Victim'. Concern over import penetration will grow as the newly industrialized Asian states show their strength and meet resistance from Japanese trade associations. In December 1982 the president of the Japan Spinners' Association, after consultations with MITI, filed with the MOF the first-ever Japanese dumping suit against a foreign nation. Japanese textile manufacturers hoped to persuade the government that South Korean cotton yarn was being sold to Japan below its domestic price. Problems were also likely to arise over steel materials. In a repetition of what European readers might regard with wry amusement, the Japanese steel industry has had to face increased imports from Brazil and South Korea, who have hopes of becoming market leaders for specific items in Japan. Ironically, too, much of the steel from Korea has come from modern plants that were built with Japanese assistance. The response of the Japanese government to strenuous overseas challenges to domestic industries that are less capable of beating off foreign competition should be interesting.

Concern for the fate of declining Japanese industries at the hands of Asian rivals is widespread and has probably made the public less enthusiastic (if this is possible) over extending technological assistance to potential competitors. Fears of industrial lethargy also have other roots. The phrase 'English disease' is part of Japanese contemporary folklore. It appears to represent two unfortunate features of Western industrialization that the public thinks Japanese society would do well to avoid. The advantages of late development in a homogeneous nation have led to a general complacency that Japan will be able to prevent the twin evils of excessive welfarism and major social fragmentation that are regarded as prevalent in Britain. The *Yomiuri* newspaper, for example, greeted 1984 by announcing that while it stood for equality of opportunity it was less enthusiastic over egalitarianism if this might damage the will to work. Those who support a wider debate on alternative goals to economic growth have made little headway in postwar Japan. Fears of eventual economic decline often appear merely to encourage a greater pursuit of affluence. Many comment on the dangers of an ageing Japan, but since the date predicted for this apparent breakdown in the existing social security system is 2025, it is again a little difficult to take these predictions seriously.

Those, such as Daniel Bell, who have asked what might happen to Japan if growth were to falter or lose its appeal can only be answered by noting that neither is yet likely. The MOF has coined the impossible neologism 'softnomics' to describe what it sees as a shift in consumer expenditure in favour of services over goods and to encourage the private sector to satisfy better what the ministry regards as a significant change in purchasing patterns. This, it needs to be stressed, does not necessarily presage any decline in economic activity, but rather a change in direction. More (better) language schools and fewer cars might not be a bad idea. Lucky the nation that can entertain such thoughts, without having to concern itself with the more mundane world of 13% unemployment or negative productivity rates. Japanese society has its critics, but few would commence an account of its problems with the chapter heading, 'An Economy that No Longer Performs' chosen by Lester Thurow to describe the United States' present condition.

The past is not necessarily prologue. Historians have a vested interest in suggesting that their work may provide a guide to the future, but in their less-guarded moments some might admit that events frequently catch everyone out. To suggest that Japan will remain a stable society underpinned by a respectable growth rate for the remainder of this decade is little more than a guess, though one based on recent developments and extrapolations. Should any such estimation be accepted, additional factors ought also to be added to place this prospect in better light. First, it is likely that Japan's economic performance will continue to outpace that of most of its rivals. Secondly, any growth of this magnitude by Japan would take place in an economy very much larger than it was a generation or even a decade ago. An annual growth rate of 9% for 1961–71 is less of an achievement than 4% in 1984. It might also be folly to assume too easily that there are set limits to growth, which will inevitably curtail the future Japanese economy. It did, after all, confound the prophets in the 1970s when its rivals had expected that the repercussions from the oil shocks would stall the giant. There are grounds for a degree of optimism over Japan's prospects, if trade wars can be avoided overseas and the service sector's more advanced technological parts are able to propel the domestic economy forward.

There are straws in the wind to support the optimists' case. Part of this is the psychological approach of some in government and industry to confront the future rather than treat it as something to be avoided until it creeps up on one. The fears of Europeans that the 21st century will not be to their liking contrast unfavourably with the rash of symposia already under way in Japan on the possible characteristics of the next century. Universities, research centres and the media are eager to think about technological change and assess its social impact. Japan, of course, is not about to de-industrialize or switch its investment patterns drastically because of new generation computers or optical fibre communications, but it does wish to champion such products and consider their consequences. Shaping the 'information society', however, will have its problems. The bureaucratic rivalry between MITI and the Post and Telecommunications ministry over control and access to government data has yet to be patched up, enterprises may be reluctant to commit themselves to invest in office and factory automation, and the wider public may be sceptical of structural changes that put their jobs at risk.

Can the economic and social issues be solved? The spokesmen for the new technology would give a cautious but affirmative answer to the doubters. Their claim that Japan is capable of leading the switch to computers and information rests on the present quality of Japanese research, the argument that if Japan hesitates its trade competitors will take the crown and confidence that Japanese management will be able to retrain rather than replace those members of the work-force likely to see their present jobs taken over by automation and robots. This may be the case, but any successes in these new fields can only be at the expense of other industrial nations. While the technological changes may be digestible over time for Japanese society, they could introduce yet another unwelcome dimension to the seemingly endless saga of trade friction with Japan's international rivals.

What is the current state of the Japanese economy? How is it likely to fare over the rest of this decade? Such questions attract immense interest in Japanese circles and increasingly abroad. First the position today. The economy entered 1984 in surprisingly good shape, thanks to improvements in the United States which led to an export boom of Japanese products that more than compensated for what until recently had been sluggish domestic demand. Although commentators could point to a host of potentially serious issues, such as the large trade surplus and the gross undervaluation of the yen, there is reason to believe that Japan's own recovery is now firmly under way. The 3.4% growth rate for fiscal 1983 that had been predicted by the government is likely to be revised as the economy picks up. The Economic Planning Agency's announcement in the summer of 1983 that the three-year recession from March 1980 to February 1983, caused by the second oil shock, was over, quickly proved correct as the longest postwar downturn was replaced by a patchy recovery. Some economic forecasters have hopes of 4% economic growth in fiscal 1984.

Japan, it would seem, has left the lower-growth period associated with the oil shock years behind it. This is both good and bad news for its competitors. An expanding Japanese economy, obviously, presents a larger potential market for foreign exporters, while Japan out of recession is more likely to boost domestic consumption and pay (perhaps) less attention to capturing yet more export contracts. We ought not to be surprised, however, if Japan confounds its observers by increasing still further its exports and receives in return yet more adverse overseas criticism. The probability, if past experience can be taken as any guide, is that Japanese imports may stage a modest increase, while its exports will climb at a considerably faster pace on the back of the brisk American and slower European advances.

The explanations for Japan's likely continued success are broadly twofold. We might divide our account simply into domestic factors behind Japanese growth and the current international scene. First, the present state of the Japanese economy. Growth today, as in the past two generations, has depended on a strong manufacturing base. Investment, it is true, is not at the levels of the 1950s and 1960s, but new plants have been constructed and can be interpreted as indications of a degree of confidence in the future. Technological innovations on the scale of the immediate postwar years are indeed missing, but this is hardly a problem unique in Japan. In addition to a willingness to invest, management has been able to retain the trust of labour in a period where wage demands were moderate and, as a consequence, inflation was remarkably low. The ability of both sides of industry to co-operate in a period when Japan faced a quadrupling of oil costs has been a vital factor behind Japan's resilience. Real wage rates have hardly increased but the runaway inflation registered by the consumer price index in the mid 1970s appears to have left its mark on the public. A determination not to become involved in a captive wage–price spiral suggests that labour and management negotiations are, in effect, part of an unofficial incomes policy.

Such a scheme is made easier by the annual arrangements for pay bargaining. Union federations announce publicly their wage goals for the coming year in January and then attempt to reach a settlement with the employers by the spring. The wage increase negotiated by the steel industry frequently serves as a guideline to others. The government's role is important since it is itself a large employer (the biggest single union in Japan is the federation of local public workers' union with 1.27 million members) and is expected to take note of recommendations from the National Personnel Authority with regard to government employees' pay and conditions of service. But the most important direct labour–management talks take place in the larger private enterprises. Here the two sides meet regularly to achieve a settlement. Management needs the co-operation of its entire labour force and is rarely confronted with separate bargaining units for different professions or crafts. Most large corporations possess one enterprise union that is empowered to negotiate for everybody. In smaller firms unionization, as we saw earlier, is far less prevalent. Strikes are usually of a short duration and have declined sharply, as has been the case in Europe since the mid 1970s. Only West Germany of the main capitalist nations has a better record over labour disputes. It alone suffered fewer stoppages or lost fewer man-days in 1980 than Japan.

All this should not be taken to imply that unions in Japan are the puppets of management and can be coerced into obedience. Unions, thanks to the encouragement of SCAP's Labour Division, gained immense power during the occupation that neither the companies nor successive conservative governments have been in a position to alter substantially. The contrast between this and the slow gains and reverses of the British trades union movement is stark. Professor Dore has put it this way: 'Japanese industry has had its social democratic revolution whereas British industry has not.' He sees the two fundamental gains for Japanese unionism as 'the unquestioning acceptance of the union as a legitimate bargaining agent in matters of wages and the protection of persons, with rights to full facilities within the factory to do its legitimate job' and 'the abolition of all but monetary distinctions between the formerly separate "statuses" of staff and manual workers'. Unionization is part of the fabric in larger Japanese companies. The unions cannot be wished away; the closed-shop rules. Yet there have to be reservations. Japanese industrial relations are less antagonistic, in part, because of the rights that unions have had secured for them and also because some of the harsher medicine can be handed out to subcontracting firms and part-timers who are not unionized. The co-operative nature of much unionism in Japan has been assisted by the postwar political and economic climate and the dualism of the system. The union song of Japan's largest electrical manufacturers refers both to the 'century of the working man arrives!' and 'Our Hitachi! Hitachi where the muscles tense!'

A decade ago many observers were eager to predict the state of Japan in the 1980s. Some of these social scientists felt that an ageing labour force, the difficulties of augmenting earlier productivity increases and the more widespread pursuit of leisure would present major difficulties for the future Japanese political economy. Disruptions, we were told, would lead to 'politicization, privatization, and alienation'. It is clear that from the vantage point of 1984 many of these guesses have come badly unstuck. A sense of national crisis during the 1970s had the reverse effect. Scarcity of resources and international criticism of Japanese trading behaviour probably worked to ease the domestic situation. When sacrifices were called for, nearly half of the electorate stuck with the LDP. Politics was not seen to have become a zero-sum game. The ruling party might not be popular but it knew how to steal the opposition's clothes and claim the welfare state as its own. Dissatisfaction was not sufficiently strong for political parties supported by labour federations to make any substantial headway. Unionization of the work-force by the end of 1983 was at its lowest level since the occupation authorities had encouraged the postwar rebirth of labour activity. Wage demands were moderate and the employers' response was frequently to reduce them still further.

Two central factors bearing on continued Japanese growth have been the value of the yen and the relatively free nature of international trade that has permitted the steady flow of its exports. The Japanese government has certainly come under considerable foreign criticism for its behaviour in both of these areas but, as of 1984, it had stuck to its guns. Had Japan benefited by bending the rules? Or had the Japanese public grounds for believing that the 'rules' applied only to their nation? The popular answer in the West to these questions can hardly be in doubt. Stories emerge of senior Japanese representatives whose attempts to rebuff European charges of manipulated exchange rates and closed markets are listened to with barely contained mirth at international conferences. The syndicated American humorist Art Buchwald spoke for many when, in his list of predictions of what his readers would not hear in 1984, wrote of the Japanese minister who could say: 'Japan can no longer export more than it imports without upsetting other nations' balance of trade. We are therefore lifting all restrictions on foreign goods, so other countries may compete fairly in the marketplace.'

First, the subject of international trade that inevitably features in most discussions of contemporary Japan. Japan has a large overall balance of payments surplus. It is not, of course, the only nation to be in such a fortunate position, but many critics remain convinced that this achievement has been accomplished through encouraging exports and by both formal and informal restrictions on imports. The charges have increased as the European and North American economies continued to flounder. The arguments of both sides have by now become thoroughly predictable. The EC repeats that the Japanese market is, in effect, closed through use of a series of bureaucratic devices that contradict the assurances of the Japanese government that all is well. The shouting match goes on.

The Research Institute of National Economy has estimated that for the 1983 fiscal year Japan's exports will increase by over 7% and that imports will decrease by 2%. The results of such an imbalance will be an increase in overseas criticism and repeated Japanese statements that the government and its agents are doing all within their power to encourage Japanese companies and consumers to look more favourably on foreign goods. What is more disturbing, however, is the probability that such balance of payments surpluses will persist throughout the 1980s and possibly beyond. Predictions have been made by the Japan Economic Research Centre that suggest the growth potentiality of the Japanese economy is still very considerable and that the setbacks of the 1970s will be overcome by relatively rapid growth over the next decade. The problem of a large deficit with the oil-producing nations and an even larger surplus with other industrial and developing states is not about to disappear. An estimated trade surplus of $33 billion for 1983 and $45 billion for 1984 may be taken as perhaps typical of the range of statistics that will be headlines in the financial pages of the press in the future. The strengths of the economy that make this unwelcome news for Europe and North America will remain the preparedness of industrialists to invest, the co-operative nature of labour and the certainty of technological advances for Japan that will either flow from its own research centres or be imported from abroad under licensing agreements. Machinery will still be Japan's chief export in 1990, though the type of machinery exported will gradually change as robots and office machinery gain in importance. Japanese trading companies and their industrial partners will also capture more large construction contracts for entire 'turnkey' plants in southeast Asia and the Middle East. The technological factor in the future Japanese economy will be of considerable importance. The Japan Economic Research Centre has suggested that out of a growth potentiality of 5% for the 1980s some 3% is attributable to technological factors that will inevitably increase productivity. The remaining 2% may be shared by labour and capital.

No combination of features will be able to succeed without an improvement in Japan's own domestic economy. Critics within Japan have been arguing that their government has long relied too heavily on exports to generate growth rather than letting domestic demand have its head. The LDP has, however, got itself into a difficult spot over economic policy. Since it has called for administrative reform to stem the need to continually increase the amount of government bonds required to finance the national deficit, it can hardly spend its way out of the present position. Massive public-works schemes may gradually become a thing of the past – certain rural areas such as Niigata perhaps excepted. Rather than encourage the expansion of the economy by monetary or fiscal measures, the cabinet is optimistic that demand will pick up by itself. Numerous economists have expressed doubts over this. Should the domestic sector fail to make any substantial improvement, the temptation to boost exports still further would seem to be unavoidable.

The Japanese government has a number of ripostes that it will make to the many overseas critics of Japan's balance of payments policy. Its principal argument has long been that Japan badly needs its current account surplus with the majority of the industrial nations to offset its large deficit with its oil and other natural-resource suppliers. Japan's successful efforts to economize over fuel, the cheaper price of oil by 1983 and the probability that oil and raw materials will slowly become less important as alternative energy sources are developed and food-stuffs become a smaller item in an affluent nation's budget may go some way to lessening these assertions. The government's case, however, remains, and will continue to remain, that Japan's dependency on natural resources necessitates its present trading policies. It is difficult to disagree. It ought to be recalled that until the late 1960s Japan had a balance of payments deficit owing to the size of its import bill and little sympathy was then heard from other industrial nations on Japan's predicament. A country whose imports of oil increased in cost from $4 billion to over $20 billion between 1972 and 1974 can hardly escape a strong sense of vulnerability. This unease prevails throughout Japanese society. It, doubtless, leads to the presentation of an exaggerated case on many occasions and presumes excessively on foreign understanding and sympathy, but the core of Japan's thesis is sound. It needs a large surplus on the export of finished goods to compensate for its essential imports.

Two additional arguments have frequently been employed by Japanese spokesmen when their government is under attack for its trade surplus. First, it is not always noted in the Western media that Japan runs a substantial deficit on its long-term capital account. In 1981 this amounted to $13.6 billion and projections for the future have suggested that it might reach $25 billion by 1986. These figures weaken somewhat the charge that Japan favours its own shippers for transporting its imports or that its tourists invariably fly on Japanese carriers. Most of this deficit is on travel and transport services. The idea that Japanese industry is a 'copycat' that has to pay out large amounts on the import of foreign technology is also no longer correct, since it receives greater royalties on new technological agreements than it is obliged to pay to import know-how. The second factor, which may also be overlooked, is the rapid increase in capital transfers from Japan to overseas. This inevitably reduces the size of the Japanese balance of payments surplus and enlarges the role of Japan in the international economy. The motives for the export of Japanese capital have varied. In part, they stem from the calculations of industrialists that more labour-intensive firms have little choice but to set up factories overseas or go out of business. Increases in labour and other costs have made many of the types of enterprises that Japan knew in the 1950s quite uneconomical today. The majority of companies in this category have selected sites in south-east Asia and operated under some form of joint-venture arrangement with substantial local management and capital. The technological level in many of these schemes may not be high and has been the cause of overseas criticism that Japan is careful to ration the export of its knowledge. There are also doubts in Asia over the behaviour of Japanese management and its general reluctance to involve itself in the local society. This feeling of Japanese aloofness, aided by separate schools and facilities for expatriate staff, has not helped in the creation of a new relationship to replace the bleak memories of the occupation years.

Aside from market and resource calculations behind the construction of manufacturing and extractive industries in southeast Asia, Japan has recently begun to invest in the European and American arena from somewhat more complex motives. The government is well aware that to preserve its existing share of these markets from political pressures to limit Japanese exports requires prompt action. Yet, while this was obviously in the interest of the Japanese government and its trade policies, it has not been easy to persuade major Japanese corporations to invest in expensive manufacturing plants in advanced industrial nations. The Tokyo representative offices for many American states and the EC's permanent delegation are in competition to entice Japanese corporations to their particular region. It is a seller's market. The opening of quite small companies in the United States or the labour practices of Japanese firms in Britain can be guaranteed to attract favourable publicity in the host country in the light of continuing high unemployment in the West. In the case of Europe, a considerable portion of Japan's investment has been in Britain, because of the language difficulties elsewhere and the financial advantages that London may possess. However, as of early 1984, the much heralded prospect of

Nissan building a car factory in Britain had yet to be realized. The delays and uncertainties over this project reflect both differences of opinion within Nissan and the difficulties of reaching agreement within Britain over the terms and conditions that could be offered to the Japanese company. The Federation of Japanese Automobile Workers' Unions and representatives from rival British firms have put considerable pressure on their respective governments to either cancel or scale down the proposed plant. The Japanese unionists claim to fear that a factory in Britain would take jobs away from their members, while British enterprises are hoping to persuade the government that any eventual plant must have a high level of local content from the outset. Should an announcement that agreement had been reached by all parties be made, it would confirm the seriousness of Japanese industry's determination to manufacture its products in Europe. It would also be taken as evidence that both the Japanese government and its industrialists recognize the dangers of growing protectionist feelings.

Political realities have played an important part, too, in persuading Japanese car manufacturers to commence constructing plants in the United States. By the 1980s it was clearly essential for Japan to prove its intentions in a substantial manner. It would no longer be sufficient to show its goodwill merely by funding US–Japan trade research centres or by donations to the Detroit symphony orchestra. The tentative approval in December 1983 by the United States federal trade commission (the voting was 3–2 in favour) for the joint venture between General Motors and Toyota to assemble small cars in California cleared the way for one important initiative. Since Honda was already in production in Ohio and Nissan was underway in Tennessee it could be said that Japanese car manufacturers were prepared to invest substantial sums in order to retain a valuable market share. There were some, however, in the American car industry who now recognized that the Japanese advantages in the small car market might lead Japanese car manufacturers in Nagoya and Tokyo to consider moving upmarket. The implications for the future of an American industry, which by 1984 was only beginning to regain health after some disastrous years, were far from reassuring.

The wish to be seen to be upholding the free-market system over imports is necessary for Japan if its trading successes are to escape severe restrictions from other nations. This, however, has proved a difficult task for successive Japanese governments. There is a strong and seemingly persistent feeling in the West that obstacles remain.

Occasionally this has been recognized by Japanese spokesmen, but the more frequent recourse has been to point out the lack of import restrictions on most goods and to claim that even Japanese embassies and organizations (such as Japan External Trade Organization) work actively to dispel misapprehensions on the supposedly closed nature of the Japanese market. The gap persists. The former Japanese ambassador to Washington, Ushiba Nobuhiko, admitted in an interview in January 1984 that his country 'tends to announce impressive policy goals but does not necessarily follow through on them'. He and many other critics see the fault as lying within the Japanese bureaucracy. Rival agencies are reluctant to surrender long-held powers or willing to discourage overzealous customs officers from excessive obstructionism. Rightly or wrongly, red tape is felt to ensnarl the foreign trader or manufacturer. There would appear to be no likely meeting of minds over these informal trade barriers. Japanese bureaucrats will not be easily persuaded to alter their behaviour, while the Western businessman will remain impatient in front of what he may regard as measures designed specifically to keep him out of the marketplace.

The Japanese government has greater problems, however, over its agricultural policies. It can accurately point out that the EC is not exactly a believer in a free market either in its attitude towards supporting inefficient hill farmers and wine growers, but the complaints here come largely from the United States. Washington, in the face of domestic complaints, has long wished for Japan to dismantle more of the quotas and tariffs that restrict beef and citrus imports. Japanese academics and journalists, while agreeing that Tokyo certainly has a poor case for a nation that professes to believe in open markets, note that any substantial liberalization of agriculture would probably lead to greater competition from other exporters and that Texas and California might be surprised by the results. Without the present national quotas Americans might lose out to challenges from Australian meat and Brazilian oranges. The total opening up of the Japanese market is most improbable in the 1980s and any gains that the United States may gradually make in increasing its agricultural exports will make little dent in its trade imbalance with Japan. This does not excuse Japanese tactics, but, until such time as its farmers can be persuaded to diversify and the political consequences of over-representation of rural Japanese constituencies in the Diet have been tackled, the negotiations can be assumed to continue at their present snail's pace.

The conviction that the yen was substantially undervalued appeared widespread by 1984. President Reagan and Prime Minister Nakasone had agreed in Tokyo in the autumn of 1983 to institute a joint investigation of the issue, but even before the study group could reach any tentative conclusions critics were quick to step in with their own opinions. Witnesses to the House of Representatives' Banking Committee claimed that a broad range of American and Japanese business leaders and economists believe the yen–dollar rate should be in the neighbourhood of ¥200 to the dollar or stronger, and others, such as the chairman of Caterpillar Tractor Co., complained that major Japanese rivals in world markets had gained a 25% price advantage through Japanese central bank manipulation of the yen. But the charges and rebuffs were harder to disentangle once attempts were made to ascribe responsibility for the yen's weaknesses. Was this really a case of Japan rigging the market or more the result of continuing high American interest rates? Was a weak yen necessarily in Japan's best interests? Why, if the accusations against Japan were correct, did the yen continue to gain against European currencies?

Both sides could point to factors in their favour. Many suggested that the large United States federal budget deficit was the real villain of the piece since it had led inevitably to higher interest rates in order to attract money from overseas to finance the shortfall. The rise of the dollar, since the decision of the Federal Reserve Board in October 1979 to tighten the money supply and permit interest rates to fluctuate, has led, according to this school, to a corresponding weakening of the yen that may persist, despite Japan's balance of payments surplus, until American interest rates begin to fall. The Japanese vice-minister of finance for international affairs has stated that, so long as the interest rate gap persists, it will be difficult to correct the value of the yen. This may well be accurate but it is open to question whether he was being totally accurate when he said outsiders were 'mistaken' in imagining that Japanese officialdom had intervened to keep the yen low.

The sceptics insisted that the role of the Japanese government could not be ignored. Several bankers and financial journalists in Britain and the United States have long felt that the system whereby Japanese government bonds are placed with banks and security companies at artificially low rates of interest has influenced the behaviour of the yen. Others have gone further and said that the Bank of Japan does enter the market – it would be surprising if it did not on occasion – and influences the purchasing patterns of trading companies and institutional buyers. Such practices suggest that the Japanese government is in a position to correct part of the problem if it should so wish. By retaining a strong hold on all interest rates within Japan, it has encouraged an outflow of funds and contributed to the present misalignment of interest rates. Calls for interest rates to be fixed by the market are likely to grow, within as well as outside Japan, but the financial authorities will move only slowly to alter a structure that divides up the type of loans that different banks are permitted to grant. Liberalization is not around the corner. The days of the highly segmented financial system that kept city banks, long-term banks and regional groups off each other's preserve will change only slowly. The ties between the MOF and the smaller, less competitive banks remain close and may prevent a free-for-all.

What other weapons are left in the armoury? How might the Japanese government react? Gradual relaxation of government restrictions on the flow of capital into and from Japan ought to strengthen the yen. Since most exchange controls were abolished in 1980 it might be thought that there would by now be a free movement of capital. This, unfortunately, is not the case. Japanese individuals and institutions are not free to borrow or lend at will, since their government imposes quotas on external loans by Japanese banks and discourages its own citizens from earning higher interest from other sources than the derisory amounts on offer from the high street banks. Yen bonds issued in Tokyo by foreign borrowers are important, but European bonds (issued outside Japan in yen) are far less significant and are watched by the authorities. The Bank of Japan and MOF appear not to wish to encourage moves to increase the role of the yen as an international currency. Any action in this direction would inevitably weaken MOF direction of Japan's financial markets and make for responsibilities that the government would rather leave to others. (Only 37% of Japan's exports in 1982 and a mere 2% of its imports in 1981 were denominated in yen. This will not be expected to increase unless given official encouragement.)

A number of commentators thought the introduction of overseas complaints over the yen little more than the rehashing of a very old story by the United States. The suspicion that the issue was brought up in the light of the seemingly intractable American trade deficit with Japan appears correct. Given the remarkably high Japanese savings rates, any slow liberalization of Japan's finance markets may not go far to altering the yen's value or restraining a highly competitive trading nation. It might be more realistic to accept that Japan is likely to progress throughout the 1980s and beyond with a continuation of the recent successes that have made almost monotonous reading for jaded Europeans. Nor could the United States be satisfied with Japanese forecasts that suggest a higher Japanese rate of growth for the 1980s than the 1970s, a lower propensity to import, but the acquisition of 25% of the North American car market by 1990, a sizeable trade balance and an appreciating yen. It would take more than a clearer American industrial policy or the creation of a Washington version of MITI to overcome the Japanese edge.

It is doubtful too whether the public in either the United States or the EC has yet come to grips with the more likely explanations for Japan's continuing advances. There was recognition of the fact that Japan produced high-quality products on a large scale, but little knowledge of the rudiments of the social organizations that manufactured these goods so successfully. Japan remained largely unknown, while those who did possess opinions frequently based them on outdated concepts. Hopes of remedying this situation appear slim. It is only on very rare occasions, such as when an American President visits Japan, that the wider public is reminded of the importance that successive administrations have placed on the US–Japanese relationship. Lacking this shared strategic interest, it is even more difficult to envisage much improvement in links between Europe and Japan. Japan has remained the preserve of the specialist. Diplomats and academics build their careers out of it. Resident businessmen and journalists alike parade their knowledge, but the trickle-down effect has been minimal. Japan is not so much misunderstood in many European eyes as still undiscovered.

Continued trade friction appears probable even if some of these predictions should be realized. An examination of the recent history of US–Japanese economic relations suggests that there has been a progression in disputes from those involving simpler to more advanced technologies. The textile wrangle of the Sato–Nixon era gave way to the steel issue (solved by the trigger price mechanism that limits Japanese steel being sold on the American market), and this in turn was superseded by consumer electronics and car difficulties. Voluntary restraint over Japanese exports of cars to the United States for the past four years has helped dampen down a major source of American managerial and labour unease. But clearly there will be more trade problems in the next decade as Japanese industry develops new technologies and the United States continues to feel itself unfairly excluded from some opportunities to sell in Japan. The present difficulties that the United States claims to face in tendering for electronic equipment orders from the Nippon Telegraph and Telephone Public Corporation (NTT) and in selling tobacco products in Japan are examples of the restrictions that may exist. It is probable too that the computer field will furnish fertile ground for additional accusations and rebuttals.

The prospects for Western direct involvement in Japan in the 1980s appear slight. Given the recent record of overseas corporations in Japan, there is little reason to suppose that such involvement will alter the trade balance between Japan and its chief industrial partners. The Japanese market is hard to enter, competition can be fierce and it may be difficult to find many products for which there are not already adequate substitutes manufactured and sold by Japanese enterprises. Some foreign firms have done well in Japan, IBM and Coca-Cola deserve mention, but others have discovered how tough the going can be and have pulled out. Not all Western companies have been prepared to make the large investments in capital and competent personnel that any serious venture in Japan requires. Non-tariff barriers there may be, but the difficulties that newcomers face in attempting to sell to very demanding wholesalers and consumers ought not to let us forget the setbacks and hostility that Japan had to overcome in getting restarted in some Western countries after the occupation.

There will continue to be periods of tension when politicians and businessmen will be tempted to overstate their cases and lay the blame elsewhere. The day of an informed public is far off. There will be repetitions of the friction in the 1970s which one senior American executive could later look back on dryly as an era when seemingly 'the leading export of both countries was excuses – Japanese excuses for lagging US investment and trade barriers, American excuses for inept promotion and marketing of US products in Japan'. To change popular attitudes will certainly be a long haul. Western faults are easier to identify and need to be corrected before there can be the basis for mutual understanding. It can hardly be said that the European public yet appreciates the Japanese challenge or the extent to which much of the Japanese economy stresses high technology and higher value-added goods that will intensify trade competition. The danger for Japan may be to ignore the implications of its economic advance and neglect the social and political consequences overseas. Some widely held Japanese attitudes towards the West could also stand re-examination. Frequently, for example, the occupation period is seen in terms of Japanese 'diligence' or 'culture' and the extraneous influences risk being neglected. The prevalence too of the view that individualism adequately summarizes Western behaviour is rarely challenged. The belief that the work ethic has been discarded in Europe and North America is an additional generalization that has legions of Japanese supporters.

8

Conclusions

Comparisons between Japan's and western Europe's postwar history are perhaps instructive. The Japanese experience has both a number of similarities and important differences from the recent past of the states that comprise a majority of the advanced industrial nations. First a few obvious points held in common by Japan and the EC. Japan is a capitalist nation that has increasingly claimed to see itself as a partner of the West. It, too, has a very substantial stake in the present international order and can be expected to assert itself more frequently as its financial and commercial might is translated into political influence in world councils. The Japanese people came late to industrialization but have obtained since the Second World War a standard of living approximately comparable to that presently enjoyed by many Europeans. The recent mass migrations from rural Japan to the factories of the Tokyo, Nagoya and Osaka conurbations parallel the labour shifts of continental Europe. The consumption patterns and leisure activities of urban Japan and the European city-dweller are not dissimilar, while the rights of labour embodied in Japanese trades union legislation and the 1947 constitution itself are clearly based on Western models. Japan's expectations of future prosperity remain only slightly dampened by recent world developments and its citizens possess a growing self-confidence that is more than a match for Europe.

Japan's political system is essentially democratic, though this does not preclude a thick vein of corruption which in one instance a former prime minister may ultimately be required to pay for misusing his office. Justice in such cases is always slow – the appeals procedure appears inordinately lengthy – but is testimony to the independence of the judiciary. Political scandals and bureaucratic infighting abound, yet the standards expected of senior civil servants are high. The Japanese police forces are paragons of virtue in comparison with their behaviour in the 1930s and could repay study in the wake of critical reports of policing from at least one major European capital.

While one can trace the shared economic and political values, there are important historical and cultural differences that illustrate divergent paths taken by Japan and Europe since 1945. Japan's loss of empire at the end of the Pacific war freed it overnight from the blood-letting and divisiveness of decolonization that would haunt other imperial powers for the next generation and beyond. The Allies' assumption of responsibility for the former Japanese empire was a blessing in disguise for Tokyo, though to surrender Manchuria's wealth could hardly be seen in that light at the time. It certainly left Japan the poorer but it had the advantage of forcing the nation to concentrate its energies and talents on domestic reconstruction and permitted it to avoid the military retreats and psychological scars common to the other powers. (The only European state to be in the same boat as Japan was Italy. It was obliged to dismantle Mussolini's Roman empire.) Japan also took pride in the consolation that it, unlike Germany, was not divided between rival powers at the end of the war, though this was a decision that largely reflected the military strengths of the United States in defeating Japan. The wartime Japanese cabinets had been anything but astute in continuing the war long past the point where resistance could change the outcome.

One additional consequence of delaying the inevitable decision to surrender was the atomic bombing of Hiroshima and Nagasaki, with the result that Japan became the first, and so far only, nation to suffer the nuclear destruction of two of its cities. The horrors of atomic attack have inevitably coloured much of Japan's present defence policy. Its government wants nothing to do with nuclear installations on its territory, though suspicions remain that United States warships may have visited Japanese ports without first off-loading their nuclear weaponry. Despite Japan's prohibitions and inhibitions (much stronger than the phrase 'nuclear allergy' might suggest), the public is not currently fearful of any threat to its sovereignty and sees no necessity to campaign in the manner of the European anti-nuclear movement.

If the problems of overseas disengagement and limits to re-armament were ultimately seen to be advantageous to Japan, so too was its basic social configuration. While the British and French stored up tensions for the future by encouraging immigration from their colonial territories, Japan could look only to its own people to man its factories and sweep its roads. Japan does have racial and social minorities that face discrimination in housing and employment, but it has been spared the extremism of the British National Front. It is not about to witness inner-city racial tensions or have to encourage guest workers to return home. Similarly, it will not know the linguistic divisions of Belgium or the separatist movements of Celtic Britain or Corsica. The religious and political strife of Ulster is remote from the Japanese experience. Homogeneity has had its advantages. Without the slightest wish to move towards a less monolithic society, Japan does not need royal commissions or presidential reports on national goals. Dissatisfaction there certainly is, but economic growth inevitably goes some way to containing such sentiment. Any eventual change in government by some combination of parties within a centralist coalition would probably continue with the economic priorities of the postwar decades. Slicing up an expanding pie to a different formula ought not to prove impossible.

Japan today is a nation of dominant women (within the confines of the family), petty bureaucrats, civility, massive complacency and shrill criticism, incessant noise and, above all else, wealth. The working week may be five and a half days and holidays still short, but a nation where over half the honeymoons are taken overseas must be doing something right. If problems certainly exist over housing, universities and the distribution system, the Japanese people would be less than human not to take pride in their postwar achievements. International attention on Japan's economic management, its industrial relations, public secondary education and long-distance transportation network testifies to Japan's energy and effort. Some of the foreign praise may be misdirected, but who in 1945 would have prophesied that a nation with a lower per capita income than Malaya would later witness an endless procession of overseas politicians and observers intent on observing Japan's progress? Two generations ago the commentators and advisers came to Japan to instruct rather than learn. The process has since been largely reversed. Japan today is no earthly paradise, but it has earned a measured round of applause. Its people have certainly never had it so good when compared with the authoritarianism and misery of the war years. When all the qualifications have been made and the reservations noted, the credit ultimately belongs to the Japanese state and its citizens. Fortune and friends have played their part, but they do not account for more than a portion of the result. Pain and national pride have been the real spur. Contemporary Japan has won its way back and more.

Appendix

Prime Ministers of Japan (1946–89)

22 May 1946*	Yoshida Shigeru
22 May 1947	Katayama Tetsu
10 Mar. 1948	Ashida Hitoshi
15 Oct. 1948	Yoshida Shigeru
10 Dec. 1954	Hatoyama Ichiro
28 Dec. 1956	Ishibashi Tanzan
25 Feb. 1957	Kishi Nobusuke
19 July 1960	Ikeda Hayato
9 Nov. 1964	Sato Eisaku
7 July 1972	Tanaka Kakuei
9 Dec. 1974	Miki Takeo
24 Dec. 1976	Fukuda Takeo
7 Dec. 1978	Ohira Masayoshi
17 June 1980	Suzuki Zenko
27 Nov. 1982	Nakasone Yasuhiro
6 Nov. 1987	Takeshita Noboru
2 June 1989	Uno Sousuke
9 August 1989	Kaifu Toshiki

*Date of initial cabinet formation
Source: *Asahi Shinbunsha, Asahi Nenkan, 1988*

Bibliography

(Most of the works below are available in paperback)

General texts

Beasley, W. G., *The Modern History of Japan* (London, 1973)
Kodansha Encyclopedia of Japan (Tokyo, 1983; supplement, Tokyo 1986)
Reischauer, Edwin O., *The Japanese Today* (Cambridge, Mass., 1988)
Storry, G. R., *A History of Modern Japan* (Harmondsworth, 1978)

History

Daniels, Gordon, and Drifte, Reinhard (eds.), *Europe and Japan: Changing Relationships since 1945* (Ashford, Kent, 1986)
Dower, John W., *Empire and Aftermath: Yoshida Shigeru and the Japanese Experience, 1878–1954* (Cambridge, Mass., 1979)
Eto Jun, *A Nation Reborn* (Tokyo, 1974)
Ienaga Saburo, *The Pacific War* (New York, 1978)
Kano Tsutomu (ed.), *The Silent Power* (Tokyo, 1976)
Lehmann, Jean-Pierre, *The Roots of Modern Japan* (London, 1982)
Livingston, Jon, Moore, Joe and Oldfather, Felicia, *The Japan Reader 2, Postwar Japan: 1945 to the Present* (Harmondsworth, 1976)
Maruyama Masao, *Thought and Behaviour in Modern Japanese Politics* (London, 1969)
Mendl, Wolf, *Issues in Japan's China Policy* (London, 1978)
Scalapino, Robert A. (ed.), *The Foreign Policy of Modern Japan* (Berkeley, 1977)
Welfield, John B., *An Empire in Eclipse* (London, 1988)
Wilkinson, Endymion, *Misunderstanding Europe vs. Japan* (Tokyo, 1981)
Yoshida Shigeru, *The Yoshida Memoirs* (London, 1961)

Politics

Baerwald, Hans H., *Party Politics in Japan* (Boston, 1986)
Destler, I. M., Clapp, Priscilla, Sato Hideo and Fukui Haruhiro, *Managing an Alliance* (Washington, D.C., 1976)
Inoguchi Takashi and Okimoto, Daniel I. (eds.), *The Political Economy of Japan*, vol. II, *The Changing International Context* (Stanford, Cal., 1988)
Itoh Hiroshi, *Japanese Politics – An Inside View* (Ithaca, 1973)
Johnson, Chalmers, *MITI and the Japanese Miracle* (Stanford, 1982)
McNelly, Theodore, *Politics and Government in Japan* (Boston, 1972)
Murakami Hyoe and Hirschmeier, Johannes (eds.), *Politics and Economics in Contemporary Japan* (Tokyo, 1983)
Richardson, Bradley M., *The Political Culture of Japan* (Berkeley, 1974)
Shiratori Rei (ed.), *Japan in the 1980s* (Tokyo, 1982)
Stockwin, J. A. A., *Japan: Divided Politics in a Growth Economy* (London, 1982)
Thayer, Nathaniel B., *How the Conservatives Rule Japan* (Princeton, 1969)
Yamamura Kozo and Yasuba Yasukichi (eds.), *The Political Economy of Japan*, vol. I, *The Domestic Transformation* (Stanford, Cal., 1987)

Economics

Austin, Lewis (ed.), *Japan: The Paradox of Progress* (New Haven, 1976)
Bergsten, C. Fred, and Cline, William R., *The United States–Japan Economic Problem* (Washington, D.C., 1985)
Clark, Rodney, *The Japanese Company* (New Haven, 1979)
Cohen, Stephen D., *Uneasy Partnership: Competition and Conflict in US–Japanese Trade Relations* (Cambridge, Mass., 1985)
Denison, Edward F. and Chung, William K., *How Japan's Economy Grew So Fast* (Washington, D.C., 1976)
Dore, Ronald, *Land Reform in Japan* (London, 1959)
Dore, Ronald, *British Factory – Japanese Factory* (Berkeley, 1973)
Hanami Tadashi, *Labour Relations in Japan Today* (Tokyo, 1981)
Kamata Satoshi, *Japan in the Passing Lane* (New York, 1982)
Kitamura Hiroshi, *Choices for the Japanese Economy* (London, 1976)
Lincoln, Edward J., *Japan: Facing Economic Maturity* (Washington, D.C., 1988)
Okita Saburo, *Japan in the World Economy* (Tokyo, 1973)
Patrick, Hugh and Rosovsky, Henry (eds.), *Asia's New Giant* (Washington, D.C., 1976)
Sinha Radha, *Japan's Options for the 1980s* (Tokyo, 1983)
The Japan Economic Research Centre, *Japanese Economy in 1900 in a Global Context* (Tokyo, 1983)

Culture and society

De Vos, George A., *Socialization for Achievement* (Berkeley, 1973)
Doi Takeo, *The Anatomy of Dependence* (Tokyo, 1973)
Fukutake Tadashi, *The Japanese Social Structure* (Tokyo, 1982)
Hendry, Joy, *Understanding Japanese Society* (London, 1987)
Hibbert, Howard (ed.), *Contemporary Japanese Literature* (Tokyo, 1978)
Kaplan, David E., and Dubro, Alec, *Yakuza* (London, 1987)
Kraus, Ellis S., *Japan's Radicals Revisited* (Berkeley, 1974)
Mishima Yukio, *The Sea of Fertility*, tetralogy (Tokyo, 1972–74)
Nakane Chie, *Japanese Society* (Berkeley, 1970)
Oe Kenzaburo, *A Personal Matter* (Tokyo, 1969)
Richie, Donald and Anderson, Joseph I., *The Japanese Film: Art and Industry* (Princeton, 1982)
Tsurumi Kazuko, *Social Change and the Individual* (Princeton, 1970)
Vogel, Ezra, *Japan as Number One* (Cambridge, Mass., 1979)

Index